Where You Go, I Go
TO geoff Levy and family.

may blessings follow
you wherever you go
and whatever you do.

Jacob Eisenbach

october 25, 2017

Where You Go, I Go

THE ASTONISHING LIFE OF DR. JACOB EISENBACH, HOLOCAUST SURVIVOR AND 92-YEAR-OLD FULL-TIME DENTIST

Karen McCartney

ISBN: 1514657171
ISBN 13: 9781514657171
Library of Congress Control Number: 2015910030
CreateSpace Independent Publishing Platform
North Charleston, South Carolina

"Whither thou goest, I will go; even unto the end."

Ruth: 1:16 Ruth's words to her mother-in-law

Author's Note

L-R: Roxanne, Nia, Dr. Jacob Eisenbach, Cheryl, and author Karen. Dr. E manages a full-time practice, keeping these three ladies very busy! He recently signed another 5-year office lease. (Karen McCartney's collection)

THE TITLE WHERE YOU GO, I GO comes from the words of Jacob's younger brother Sam, who pleaded to go with him when Jacob had to go to the Nazi death train. They were orphaned Jewish teens in occupied Poland; all other family members had perished.

The events in this story are true; the information comes from many hours of fascinating interviews with Dr. Jacob Eisenbach (Dr. E).

Much of the drama in his life occurred more than 60 years ago. Memory fades and word-for-word conversations often cannot be retrieved. Fortunately, he does remember some verbal exchanges.

Where he does not, I added dialogue to keep the action on stage and avoid feeling like a history lesson. The conversations are based on his description of the mood, situation and conversational style of the people. They ring true to Dr. E, which was my measuring stick.

I researched all historical facts he gave me, such as Churchill's balloons. If I found any discrepancy, we made appropriate changes; if the details varied from source to source, I used what he gave me.

The characters in his story are real. In a few cases names were changed. Similar repetitive events were 'collapsed' into one event, such as the execution scene, which happened regularly.

Dr. E has approved the contents of the book. I hope you enjoy reading this as much as I enjoyed writing it, although for you it may take only a couple of hours, while it had me in its fascinating grip for two years.

Karen McCartney
Psychologist/Teacher/Author
Lake Forest, California
August, 2015

DEDICATION

Dr. Jacob Eisenbach
(Dr. Eisenbach's collection)

I dedicate my life story to you, Harry and David, the greatest sons one could ever have. You have been my inspiration, and added depth and meaning to my life. I also wish to remember my beloved son Mark Charles, and my grandchildren and great grandchildren who so love their grandpa. Thank you for all you are and all you do.

I further want to honor the memory of my father, Majlech Eisenbach; mother, Sara Eisenbach; sister Fela and brothers Henry and Sam, all of whom perished during the years 1938 to 1947.

Finally, I want to remember Irene, my wife and mother of my sons, now deceased. And Bebe, my angel and my second mate.

Dr. Jacob Eisenbach, D.D.S.

Table of Contents

Preface

———— ∾∾∾ ————

AMERICA WAS ABSOLUTELY DEVASTATED BY the events of 9/11 with its 3,000 victims. I still view 9/11 videos with abject horror.

Now consider this: 6 *million*, the number of Jews lost in WW II; that's roughly a 9/11-size event occurring EVERY DAY FOR FIVE YEARS. It defies imagination. Added to that, many non-Jews were victims as well, like my Catholic great aunts and uncles in eastern Poland.

The main theme here is the terrible destruction the Nazis inflicted on Dr. E, his family and their way of life, as thoroughly as when Vesuvius wiped out Pompeii. It includes his recovery, peace of mind and forgiveness, plus the almost *unbelievable* life he leads at 92. (He recently renewed his 5-year office lease. Will he really work until his late 90's or even beyond? I think *yes*. Absolutely.)

I hope this book reaches today's youths, who need to really grasp what Nazi terrorism *was*. It's bullying with a fancy name and torchlight parades. For those few who actually sport swastika tattoos or display Nazi flags, I hope they will realize swastikas are not *cool*. That ugly symbol represents an entity that bashed babies against brick walls or tossed them in the air and used them for target practice; they sold the gold from victims' mouths.

Among the young people I hope will benefit from Dr. E's and my efforts are my beloved grandchildren Kaylie, Ryan, Robert and Trevor. Also my super-gifted nephews, Ben and Peter and my sweet niece, Brittany.

This is a shout-out to Dr. E's office staff – Roxanne, Cheryl and Nia, You are like family to me. You have listened to hours of stuff, encouraged me and delivered meals to Dr. E and me while we worked after hours. Like Elvis said, *Thank you very much.*

And of course, thank you, Dr. E. for sharing so much. You are my hero. My daughters say knowing you has changed my life and given me renewed faith and a wonderful optimism.

At the risk of an Oscar-type speech, I wish to thank the following for their support: my readers -- daughters Catherine and Kristen, son-in-law Todd, aunt-in-law Sylvia; friend Lori who chauffeured me and my manuscript around, brother Merle and wife Rene for their support; my mom for sharing her memories of the era (and passing on her love of writing) and my dad from whom I got a passion for history. I wish my sister Eileen had lived to see this, but she's probably watching, surrounded by a group of doggy-spirits. Finally my own furry baby, Sugar, who was always at my side while I wrote (sometimes competing with my computer for space on my lap).

Best wishes and thank you to readers,

Karen McCartney, Author
Lake Forest, CA
August, 2015

CHAPTER 1

The Unthinkable   March, 1944

*(1) Jews from the Łódź ghetto in Poland (Dr. E's home town) are put on a
freight train for deportation. This is where he and Sam
boarded the train in sub-zero weather.*

IN MARCH, 1944, HIS 'WEDDING Invitation' from the Nazis made its terrifying appearance. Jacob read it several times. Cotton-headed, he
fell onto the couch, clutching the paper. The daylight in the room
faded to black.

'Wedding Invitation' was a euphemism for a deportation summons; in turn, 'deportation' was a euphemism for riding the Nazi train to one's death.

Gallows humor.

Jews in a country anywhere *near* Hitler in 1939 or the 1940's were walking targets, and millions of them disappeared into smoke or lay in a mound of skeletons by the time Hitler put a gun to his own head.

Jacob rubbed his forehead, his brain pounding like a blacksmith working a horse shoe. He had heard the stories. Every chance they had, railroad employees whispered bits of information and warnings to Jews not yet caught up in the net. As a result of the railroad men's candor at the risk of their lives, he knew if he answered the summons, he had a date with the gas chamber.

He paced the floor. Was his time on earth really running out? Like a wind-up clock's last few little ticks?

NO. He would not surrender. He was only twenty; he had not even lived a quarter of a century. He and his younger brother Sam had their whole lives ahead of them. They needed time, precious time to leave their mark on the world.

Sam was usually the more emotional one. He took the notice and scanned it; he grabbed Jacob with shaking hands, eyes wild and wet.

"Oh, Kuba, no." He clutched Jacob's sleeve. "I don't want to stay here alone," he cried. "What will happen?"

"Don't you worry. I won't be going on any train. You and I are going to run. Come on, get every sweater and jacket we have and let's get out of here."

Sam looked up. "Where are we going? It's below zero out there and will be dark in two hours. Shouldn't we wait until morning?" He stood rooted to the floor, disbelief replacing his tears.

"We're going anywhere we can find to hide. I'm not waiting around. Do they think I'll just show up and let them kill me? Come on now, hurry up. If you hang around here, you might get a summons, too."

The color drained from Sam's face. He turned and walked woodenly to the other end of their one-room ghetto apartment, dug around in the piles of clothing and found some warm items. "I'll take extra socks, too," he mumbled from deep within a state of shock.

"Good, and some hats or towels, something to put around our heads. Come on, now, move faster. We need to get away from here right *now*."

"I'm coming." Sam walked back, arms wrapped around a large batch of clothing.

"We can't carry all that," Jacob worried. "Let's just take these." He looked through them and chose the warmest pieces. "Oh, I almost forgot. *Food*."

He gathered some cheese, crackers, the last apple, some bread, celery, and a little bit of lard wrapped in a napkin. He hoped they wouldn't have to make lard sandwiches, but he'd bring it anyway.

"How are we going to manage all this?" Now *Jacob* was starting to panic.

"Just put the food in a sack; don't bother with the lard. I'll take the clothes," offered Sam, stirring back to life. "Should I bring pillows?"

"Pillows?" *Leave it to Sam.* "No. We'll roll up some clothes for that. Let's go, then." He put the food in a sack and got the padlock, key and their food ration cards from a drawer. Sam grabbed a picture of the family, kissed it, and studied it for a moment.

White-hot pain ripped through Jacob. *Poor Sam. How is he going to cope? He's only two years younger, but he's a couple centuries more innocent.*

Sam folded the picture and put it in his shirt pocket.

Younger brother Henry was in that photo; Jacob's mind flashed back two years when Henry contracted typhus and was in a ghetto hospital.

Stop. Right now he couldn't think about what Nazis did to Henry. It ripped his heart to pieces. *Keep moving; get out of here.*

He inhaled deeply. *God, please help us.*

With that, he went out the door with Sam right behind him.

CHAPTER 2

The Way We Were   1923-1934

*L.-R. Henry, Papa, Jacob, Fela, Mama and Sam at
the Mountain of Cherries resort. (Dr. Eisenbach's collection)*

"KUBA, I'D LIKE YOU TO be a doctor." Papa said, using Jacob's nickname.
He was on Papa's lap. He smiled at his father and using his tongue,
wiggled the front tooth that was starting to loosen.

"Let me see that" said Papa. "Oh, it won't be long now, and you'll be
getting your grown-up teeth. How do you feel about that?"

"Good," he said with a big grin.

"So, you're going to be a doctor?" Papa asked again.

"What about me?" four-year-old Sam interrupted. "What will I be? A fireman?" Sam's large brown eyes, full of youthful anticipation, studied Papa's face.

"Let me think." A warm smile spread across his face. "You love books. Maybe you'll write them; tell wonderful stories. Would you like that? You would be an *author*."

"An *author*," the boy repeated. Papa must have struck a chord. Sam gazed out the window, as if picturing future glory.

"But you're going to be a doctor because you love science. Right, Kuba?"

"Yes, Papa. I'll be a great man someday." Six year-old Jacob hopped down, as if eager to get started. "I'll do wonderful things to help people. I promise."

Papa chuckled. "You don't have to promise *me* anything. It's what you promise *yourself* that matters."

Jacob looked at him in wonder. Papa said the smartest things. He was like Wise Old Mr. Owl in little Henry's story book.

"What about me?" asked eight-year-old Fela, who had just entered the room, wearing a cheery yellow sun dress. Her face already had the features that would inspire legions of young men to try to court her. Film-star beauty, everyone said.

She put a book on the table and crawled up into her father's lap. "What shall *I* be?"

"Anything you want, Sweetheart," he said, kissing the top of her head. "As bright and sweet as you are, you'll do well in life."

"Kuba's going to be a doctor," said Sam.

"I might want to be a doctor, too. I could give people medicine at the drugstore," Fela said.

"That's a *pharmacist*, Honey."

"A *pharmacist*. That's what I meant."

Papa laughed, tilting his head back. "You're precious. You'd be a good one. Go along and play now, enjoy the rest of your day. I have to get back to the factory. I keep making excuses to stay here with you."

The children hugged him just as two-year-old Henry toddled out of his bedroom. "Me too, me too," he said, pulling on his father's coat. Papa picked him up and swung him around. "Here's your hug, little *Me-Too*."

"Honey, wait a minute," said Mama as she came out of the kitchen, drying her hands on her apron.

"Another *Me-Too?*" Papa said.

She was the dark-haired love of his life that caused him such yearning before they were married. He leaned towards her and they briefly kissed. Mama walked him to the door. "See you tonight, Sweetheart."

Jacob was born in Poland in 1923; a banner year. Exciting new developments were cropping up all over the world; a spirit of optimism was in the air.

King Tut's tomb and treasures were discovered in Egypt, and a parliamentary democracy was introduced there around the same time.

In sports, U.S. boxers Gene LaRue & Kid Pancho knocked each other out simultaneously in the ring. For baseball lovers and future glory, Yankee Stadium opened.

The traffic signal was invented by an American son of former slaves, Garrett Morgan. Film with sound was exhibited at Radio City Music Hall; the Disney Studio opened; American women could now wear trousers anywhere legally.

In Poland, the first major ocean-going ship arrived at Gdynia, the new seaport. In Germany, upstart troublemaker Adolf Hitler attempted to take over the government and failed; he was in prison.[1]

The future was bright and beckoning. Jacob's home town of Łódź was the huge planet Jupiter compared to the little Neptune- and Pluto-towns

---

1 http://en.wikipedia.org/wiki/1923

around it. A charming city in western Poland, it was a busy textile center. (The many factories would draw Hitler's attention later.) The sophisticated main streets had stately stores, evoking Wilshire Boulevard in Los Angeles. The parks boasted graceful trees and little Disneyesque birds hopping from the branches down to the lush grass, finding a morsel and fluttering back up again, music sweet as sugar coming from those little beaks.

His father owned a textile factory which produced multi-colored bedspreads, delicate window coverings and jewel-toned or snow-white tablecloths. It provided them with a good living: they had many pretty things and wonderful vacations. They lived in a lovely three-bedroom apartment, but did not own a car. Only the ultra-rich had houses and cars.

Each time Papa brought home the latest product Mama was thrilled; she'd busy herself finding just the right place for it. Their apartment was furnished beautifully and lovingly; a princess would be right at home.

When Jacob's parents met, Majlech (Papa) was instantly smitten but the other half of the couple (Jacob's mother Sara) wasn't on board. She was polite, but to Mama he was just another pesky boy who thought she was pretty. He was far more than that; he was on a *mission*. He had to have her, but to his dismay, she wouldn't indulge in conversation with him.

Finally he went to his father. "Tell me how to win her love. What am I doing wrong? Sara doesn't respond when I try to speak to her."

His younger brother Zajdel walked into the room, munching on some grapes. "What do you want to talk to her for? Girls are a nuisance." Majlech ignored him and looked back at his father.

"Just be persistent, Son. That's the best approach to anything in life. Your actions will show her what she means to you, more than words could ever do. Smile at her whenever you see her and show your confidence."

"Confidence?"

"Yes; you believe you're a good person, man enough to take care of her, don't you?"

"Yes, Papa" he said, standing a little taller.

"There you go." Majlech's father said, then looked at Zajdel. "Did your mother give you those at the store?"

"Yes," he said, his mouth full of grapes.

"I don't mind, but don't take anything without asking. Especially the candy, all right?"

"Okay" said the boy, and skipped out of the room.

"It's a challenge having a candy store and raising four boys," sighed their father. Young Majlech chuckled along with him. Little Zajdel could be stubborn and often did things the way he wanted.

Majlech put his father's advice to work and the love of his life finally returned his smile. A happy marriage and four children followed.

In Jacob's youth, the whole family often went to visit Grandma and Grandpa Eisenbach at the candy store, a 15-minute walk. Sometimes Mama stayed home, not feeling well because of her heart problems; other times the children went without either parent. After these visits, Fela and the boys always came home with fruit and candy, and best of all, feeling loved and cherished.

Jacob was self-reliant. He walked alone to Hebrew preschool every day when he was four. In those days a child could do that without need for a nation-wide search afterward. The next year Mama took him to a female dentist. She had a drill that was operated by a foot pedal. Jacob stared at that, thinking of the mad scientist's laboratory he had seen in an American movie.

He took a deep breath and hopped up into the chair. He felt no pain while she worked on him. He was a tough little guy. After that visit, he always went there by himself.

They didn't cook from sundown Friday to sundown Saturday because *Shabbat* was a day of prayer. On Fridays, Mama prepared *cholent* (a traditional Jewish stew) in a huge pot, a thick mixture of turkey, duck, sausage, potatoes, carrots – the works.

Jacob and Sam were carrying it to the bakery as usual one Friday evening. Each had a handle of the giant kettle.

"Hold your end up better than that," Jacob snapped at Sam. Like many older brothers, he could be a little bossy.

"I *am*" Sam huffed. "You're dropping *your* side." Like many younger brothers, Sam could toss it right back.

They carried it into the bakery where it would be placed overnight in the oven, which was still hot.

"We'll pick it up tomorrow at noon," Jacob called as they left. Saturday was always a more amiable trip, looking forward to eating the cholent; it put them in the seventh level of heaven.

One rainy Monday morning when Jacob was eleven, he was putting on boots at the front door.

"Make sure you don't lose your hat," said Mama, hovering over him. "And can you help Henry with his boots? He's having trouble. Thank you, dear. I have to go check the stove."

Every day they walked to school and back, whatever the weather. School was easy for Jacob, he enjoyed learning, loved the challenge of math and reveled in the new discoveries in science.

Fela was clearly gifted and Sam was also; he read hundreds of books. Henry hadn't fully bloomed yet, because he was only seven; though he meant no harm, he *was*, however, extremely clever at ways to frustrate his older brothers.

Jacob watched him slosh along in puddles on the way to school. "Don't get your pants all wet. You know, I think you got your personality from Uncle Zajdel."

Henry looked up at him, rain drops all over his face, and said "What's a personality? Doesn't Uncle Zajdel need it anymore? Why'd he give it to me?"

"I don't even know how to answer that," laughed Jacob. "Just stay out of the puddles, will you?"

One day Jacob stopped by his favorite aunt's apartment to deliver a package from Mama. He had to step around all the piles of socks; this home was a sock factory. His cousins all got in the act, helping with production.

"Where is Aunt Esther?" he asked.

"In town, getting thread and yarn," his cousin answered, eyeing the package.

"Give her this from Mama." Jacob pushed aside a pile of socks on the table and put it down. "It's those extra muffin tins she wanted." He noticed some tasty-looking cheese on the counter top. He couldn't resist taking a little with him.

"Tell her thanks for the cheese," he said as he went out the door. The cousins waved happily at him, looking forward to their mama's home-baked muffins.

Jacob was sorry he missed Aunt Esther. She was their favorite aunt because she and Mama were very close sisters and Esther was a gentle and loving person.

For a little while longer, at least, the family would live undisturbed by the kind of panic and terror that was biding its time, waiting for them, right around the corner.

CHAPTER 3

Something Unbreakable   1923 - 1934

L-R: Jacob, Henry and Sam at the Mountain
of Cherries (Dr. Eisenbach's collection)

WISNIOWA GORA (THE MOUNTAIN OF Cherries), was a beautiful resort where the family spent every summer. They rented a house from a farmer who came and got them and all their luggage; they rode in his large horse-pulled cart.

They spent a full day bouncing along the road, listening to the clop-clop of the horse's steps, smelling the sweet wildflowers, chattering like magpies and planning adventures.

"Let's hike up the back trail tomorrow," Jacob said. "We can build a fort under that big old fir tree."

Henry's eyes lit up. "Then can we go fishing? We can stock the fort with our catch."

"You would need ice for that," Sam commented.

"We'll just eat them right away, then." Henry replied.

"How are you going to cook them?"

"On a campfire; what do you think?" Henry was getting frustrated with the inquisition. "Maybe we should just roast marshmallows."

"If you do that, I'll come and eat some," said Fela, who was already writing letters to friends.

During those summers Papa spent weekends with the family and took the bus into town every Monday for work. The boys were left to their own adventures. They raced around outdoors, played ball or chatted with girls. Jacob could find girlfriends anywhere, even on the Mountain of Cherries.

On a Sunday during one of those summers, the sky was a crystal shimmering blue. A few clouds drifted, like piles of cotton lazily moving overhead. The family was getting ready to have an outdoor lunch at their rented house. Mama wore a crisp white sundress and Papa was freshly attired and smelled of a gentleman's cologne that caused Mama to smile when he walked by.

While Mama and Fela put the food on the table, Papa and Jacob were talking.

"Do you still want the family to go to America?" Papa's eyes were all a-twinkle.

"Sure I do," said Jacob. "It's the land of great opportunity. And you know what? They don't have wars like Europe does. I'm so sick of wars."

"My, what serious thoughts," chuckled Papa. "I also like that you plan to travel. That's a good thing to do while you're young."

"I know, Papa. I'm going to see the whole world someday. I can't wait to see the Swiss Alps. Maybe I'll see a yodeler on top of one. And the pyramids! Did you know they're 5,000 years old?"

"Something like that," Papa smiled. "You be sure and send us lots of post cards. Are you going to ride a camel?"

Jacob frowned. "I might; they spit, you know." After a couple of seconds, he flashed a big grin. "Maybe I'll take a fine, big car and go in style, with a driver."

Papa's eyebrows reached for the sky. "A fancy car? In the desert? I don't know if they drive them there."

"Well, I'll find out."

Mama called out that the food was ready. Sam and Henry scurried over from the trees they were climbing. As they helped themselves to sandwiches and potato salad, Fela described the new hairstyle she wanted to try. One like Greta Garbo's with feather-light curls and a sweeping wave on the right side. "You know, like in *Grand Hotel,*" she said.

"Your hair is beautiful," said Papa, "you don't need to look like a film star. You're already a very pretty young lady. Are you sure you're only thirteen? You could be mistaken for the beautiful queen of a great country."

She laughed. "Oh, Papa; no one wants to be a queen anymore. Or even a princess."

"What do you want to be, then?"

She rolled her eyes up, deep in thought. "I think...I'd like to be a fashion designer."

"So that's what it is this week?" he laughed. "What happened to pharmacist?"

"Oh, I will do that, too."

Papa chuckled; if God assigned children to families, He had outdone Himself. Fela was a pure delight. In fact, all his children were.

After the meal, Jacob looked at the candy on the table, donated by Papa's parents from their store. "I wish I had known your parents, Mama. They died too soon."

She gave him a little smile. "Oh, Kuba. You would have loved them."

"Let's go play," interrupted Henry, a busy little seven-year-old who could barely sit through conversations.

Everyone started to get up from the table. "Wait," Papa said. "I want to get some pictures. Let me get our neighbor."

The children rolled their eyes. *Oh, no.*

"Just one or two," said Papa. He soon returned with the man from next door. Papa arranged them all around the table, then joined them. The neighbor took the picture.

"One more. Boys, come over here." He had them make a gymnastic triangle.

"Steady, now" he said. "Smile." Papa snapped an iconic picture. The triangle of boys formed a bond; something stronger than the sum of its parts, something solid. Just like their family, unbreakable...

Of course that all changed when the nightmare began.

CHAPTER 4

A Little Piece Of Heaven   1933–1934

*Jacob's beautiful older sister Fela, Papa
and Mama (Dr. Eisenbach's collection)*

"DOES HE COME FROM A land of black giants?" Henry asked, gawking at the
6'4" man with ebony skin walking in the circus parade. The children
had never seen a person of color before.

The man moved his long legs in a loose, easy-going manner, as the children stared with mouths agape. He wore a top hat and gloves and looked like he was dressed for a wedding, except for those red and white circus pants.

Mama laughed. "No, Sweetheart, he's not a giant, just tall. You know, in this world people come in many colors, sizes and shapes."

"Like the blocks in my building set."

"Yes; like that."

The circus came once a year; a parade of lions, elephants, acrobats, clowns and a marching band came down the main street. People lined the curbs, waving hats or colorful handkerchiefs. Three hundred children followed the tall man; their admiration was rewarded by big smiles from him.

The synagogues had spectacular music for the high holidays. Jacob was in his own heaven with it resounding all around him. Hearing the baritone sing was almost better than dancing with a pretty girl. Almost, but not quite; and he would know.

From a young age, girls seemed to like him. He was not afraid to look them in the eye and was a good listener. He might have thought they'd all be just like Mama. He had a lot to learn, but was a willing and *totally* delighted student.

Jacob and his friends loved American movies; his favorites were the scary ones, like *The Mystery of the Wax Museum*. They watched with huge round eyes and thumping hearts. Cringing in their seats, they grabbed the arm rests with clammy hands and sometimes covered their eyes. It seemed they might pass out with fright. It was pure rapture.

Wax Museum was so frightening the young man next to Jacob actually did topple right over in a dead faint. Another had his watch stolen and never felt it.

Just when Jacob thought he had seen everything, a woman stood up screaming. "My fur coat! Someone cut off part of my coat!" She was soon hysterical, running up and down the aisle.

Jacob said to his buddy, "How stupid do you have to be to bring that coat and leave it hanging off the back of your chair in a dark place like this?"

———

The family kept perishables in an ice box. Ice was delivered regularly in a horse-pulled truck; the horse wore blinders so he wouldn't be spooked by traffic beside him. The well-seasoned workhorse stood quietly while the ice man retrieved a big block of ice from the truck.

The children liked to walk over and look at the horse with his large brown eyes and golden main. "Good boy," they said. The gentle animal nodded his shaggy head in response and allowed his nose to be petted.

———

One day the boys were ice skating at a local rink.

"Be careful, Henry," Jacob said with gritted teeth; Henry had just plowed into another skater because he wasn't watching where he was going.

"Don't worry about it," said Henry as he shook himself off, ignoring the glare of the other skater.

"We're sorry," Jacob told the victim, who was struggling to right himself, so he gave him a hand up. "We'll watch him more closely."

Hearing that, Henry took off, leaving a disapproving Jacob behind.

Sam was bristling with nerves. "Come on, let's catch him."

They made long strides around the rink, and soon they were beside Henry, who had shorter legs.

"Haven't knocked anyone unconscious yet, have you?" Jacob raised his eyebrows at Henry.

"Of *course not*, Kuba, I'm fine," he said as he spun around in a circle. "Look what I can do."

"We know you can do that," put in Sam. "Let's see you skate safely now. Can you do *that*?"

"Don't bother me. I have things to do," Henry huffed at him. He started skating again, making tracks away from them as fast as his short legs would take him.

"That boy is a pain in my neck," said Jacob, shaking his head.

"Calm down, Kuba," said Sam. "We're here to have fun, okay?"

"Easy to say," said Jacob, "but I feel responsible for him. Let's stay close by him."

So they did, and Henry didn't run over any more hapless skaters. They went home to some of Mama's hot cocoa and spice muffins.

They often ice skated but didn't ski, although skiing in the beautiful Tatras Mountains rivaled anywhere in the world. Mama and Papa were afraid of anything risky.

"They're worried we'll break a leg without even getting to open a show," said Fela, repeating the children's private joke to her brothers and Jacob's best friend, Jack Sieradski. They were in the living room, out of earshot of adults.

"I'm surprised they don't worry about us walking to school in bad weather. We could get struck by lightning," chuckled Jacob.

"Or run over by a car," added Sam.

"Or maybe King Kong would steal us right off the street. It could happen," said his friend Jack, looking pleased with himself.

"King Kong," said Henry. "Is he real?"

"He's a myth," said Sam. "I've read all about him. Do you want to see my book?"

"Okay," said Henry, with huge eyes, no doubt imagining a giant ape accosting them.

One spring day Jacob was playing soccer with some local boys. One of them asked who his favorite player was.

"Iron Leg," he said. All the boys knew who he was. He once accidentally killed a goalie by kicking the ball into his chest so hard the man had a heart attack. When Jacob played, he imagined *he* was Iron Leg; might as well be the best.

Jacob was blessed with singing talent. Mama was sick one day and lay on the couch with no energy. Her face was drawn and so pale. If frightened him. He glanced at the window. *Isn't she getting enough air?* He wiped her face with a cool cloth, then opened the window a few inches.

She said "Would you stay with me? I'm feeling lonely today." He promptly went outside and told the other soccer players "*Sorry, today I sing for my mother.*"

"Mama, would you like me to sing?" He said as he took his place next to the couch, standing casually, like he'd seen singers do. She nodded, and he sang some of her favorite songs. She smiled at him and made his day.

"Kuba, you could sing for a living."

"Oh, Mama; I'm no song-and-dance man. I'm going to be a dentist."

"You'll be a fine one, too. You'll make me proud," she said with what little energy she had.

One glance at Mama stirred up a vortex of pain. He resolved not to worry her about anything, ever again. She was too precious to him to even think about losing her.

The fairy tale existence they lived was occasionally marred by some very ugly incidents. In 1933 his childhood was changed forever; his innocence gone at age 10. He witnessed a *pogrom*, anti-Semitic action, on the streets.

Anti-Semitism had always been around, just like other varieties of prejudice; now the emotions of Jew-haters in this area of Europe were stirred up and *set on fire* by Hitler. Angry Poles attacked and beat Jews to death with crowbars. The bloody end of those people so horrified Jacob he lost his breath and his balance momentarily; when he regained it, he hurried home in a state of shock.

The next year he saw another pogrom and didn't waste time gawking at it; he ran straight home. Papa constantly warned them to be careful when they went out. *Go in groups,* he'd tell them.

There was another thing that cast a long shadow over their peaceful fairy-tale life.

There really was a Big Bad Wolf.

His name was Adolf Hitler and he lived and breathed next door in Germany; he even nicknamed himself *Wolf.* He named his retreats and meeting places *The Wolf's Lair, The Wolf's Gorge, etc.*

Hitler had powerful plans for Germany. People in other countries hoped, prayed and tried to convince themselves he would keep his ambitions within his own borders.

Unfortunately for the world, that didn't happen; quite the opposite. While the children were splashing in rain puddles and kicking soccer balls, eating Mama's *cholent* and doing homework, the Wolf was getting ready to howl.

CHAPTER 5

A Speeding Train   1935-1937

Jacob's beloved Mama
(Dr. Eisenbach's collection)

AS VIOLENCE DOES, IT STRUCK unexpectedly one Sunday in 1935 in Jacob's neighborhood park. He was 12. People were enjoying picnics, playing checkers, reading, or walking among the sweet-smelling grass and rainbow hues of the floral gardens. The tall, slender elms stood like old gentlemen, stiff and bent in places, sighing in the breeze. A black wrought-iron fence surrounded the park. Every six feet it had thick posts that resembled castle towers. Little birds loved to perch on top of them.

Some of Jacob's friends planned to go there that day after an errand; he decided to come to the park and wait for them to turn up; maybe take them home with him for 2:00 dinner.

He watched some women walking their babies in prams, sporting the latest fashion in hats. One had a sleek feather in hers; she wore the hat angled to the side of her head.

He sat down on the grass and stretched out his legs, watching that feather go by. Shortly he began sunning his face with his eyes closed. He was interrupted by clattering and low voices behind him. He turned and saw people coming in and locking the gates. It took only seconds to focus on the crowbars in their hands.

Suddenly he was gasping for air. *I'm going to die right here.* His heart was pulsing in his throat; he gasped once more as he jumped to his feet.

He ran to the other side of the park and went over the fence like an Olympic pole-vaulter. Once he was safe, he glanced back to see the horror: the shrieks of the victims filled the air. Could no one come and help them? Where were the police? Trying to catch his breath, he shook like a reed in an earthquake.

He prayed his friends wouldn't arrive and be battered to death, while he hurried home to tell Mama. When he got there, he saw people he didn't know sitting in the living room; they appeared to be parents with three small children. Mama came out from the kitchen drying her hands, and introduced them as the Steins. They were dinner guests. Jacob greeted them and followed Mama back into the kitchen.

"They are struggling and don't have any food," she said quietly. He had seen this a number of times; Mama was very charitable. She even helped cousin Marysia with financial support while she studied pharmacology.

"They were among the Jews Hitler exiled and dropped off at the border; remember? You did meet them briefly once."

"Sure, Mama," he said as he gazed out the window at the street below them. "Where's Papa?"

"He's taking a nap." Mama went back to stirring some soup on the stove. Worried about his friends, the words came rushing out as he told her what happened at the park. She cried out, then rushed over and hugged him tightly.

She released him and looked him up and down. "Are you all right?"

"I'm fine, Mama, but my friends are going there."

"We could call the police, but probably the beasts will be gone by the time they get there. What do you want to do, Kuba?"

"Call them."

Mama wiped her hands and walked through the living room to the phone. She looked in the drawer under the phone for the number. She dialed it with shaky fingers. Jacob's stomach knotted and his forehead was sweaty. He wiped his hands on his pants.

She spoke to the police officer. He told her they would go check it out and *Thank you for calling*.

"He didn't sound very concerned," she said, frowning.

"That figures. Nobody stops these people. Why not?"

"I don't know, Sweetheart." She excused herself to the guests, who nodded with polite smiles, and led him back into the kitchen. "We have a good and kind God. He protected you; don't forget you're special to Him and He has a plan for your life. Always remember that."

"Aren't the ones that died special, too?"

Mama looked perplexed. "Of course, Kuba. We are all special to God. Maybe He just wanted some of them to be with Him now."

"Mama, what if Hitler comes here and tries to do something to us?" He glanced out the window and scanned up and down the street. "He hates Jews so much."

Mama stood quietly a few moments, then turned back to the stove. "I don't know, Sweetheart. God will just have to look after us, because no one else will. Papa doesn't think Hitler will come here." Her forehead creased into a frown as she stirred the soup.

A big, heavy rock settled in his stomach. He didn't want to worry her and he had done it anyway. Mama had Scarlet Fever as a child and her heart wasn't strong. In a cloud of guilt, he turned to leave the kitchen.

She stopped him, whispering "Kuba, if we have to leave here, Papa will lose his business. We can't do that."

"I know, Mama" he said, his head in a jumble. "Don't worry about it. I was just scared for a minute, but I'm fine. I'll go wash up for dinner now."

Everything was upside down; innocent people were dying. Evil was winning the battle; no one was trying to stop these killers. It made him crazy trying to sort things out that made no sense. He promised himself he wouldn't bother Mama anymore but hoped he could always talk to Papa.

After the meal was over and the Steins had gone, carrying left-overs, Jacob took Papa aside and described the pogrom. He was looking for sympathy and reassurance. What he got was very different.

"I told you to be careful," Papa said, eyes narrowed with worry and anger. "You can get yourself killed by underestimating these people."

"I know, Papa. I'm sorry. It was a stupid mistake; it was just so unexpected. Who would think they would come in a park and do that? There were little kids and babies in there."

Papa sighed. "Children and babies mean nothing to these people. It's best to stay on your toes, like I keep telling you. Don't put yourself in that position, Kuba. Inside a fenced area where you could have been trapped? You were alone? Don't do that. Use common sense. Always have someone else with you, the more the better."

"I promise," he told Papa, summoning his most sincere face.

Mama came out of the kitchen.

"What are we going to do with our boy?" asked Papa. "He doesn't listen to our warnings."

Oh no. Don't worry her with this, he thought miserably.

Mama first gave Papa a little kiss, then said "He'll be all right. Kuba is a survivor. He knows how to get himself out of tight situations."

Papa gave Jacob a withering look. "You're only twelve years old. I suppose you think you are invincible?"

Oh, no.

"No, Papa" Jacob said. He hated to let them down. He had to divert his father's attention. "I've got to do my homework now, so I can keep my marks high. I have a big history report to work on."

Papa was such a kind man; he wasn't comfortable letting this dangle unresolved. "I don't mean to be hard on you; I would rather die than see anything happen to you. Do we have an agreement that you'll be more cautious?" Papa extended his hand.

"Agreed." They shook hands. Papa loved him dearly or he wouldn't get so upset; Jacob knew he was loved as surely as the sun comes up in the morning.

While he worked on his report, Sam was lying on the bed watching him, snapping his fingers in his own little rhythm.

"Stop that, Sam. I can't concentrate."

"Do you have class with that geography teacher tomorrow? Your favorite one?"

"I have class with him every day," Jacob replied.

"Why do you like him so much? Is he easy?"

"No, he's not easy; he tells us hilarious stories of traveling in each country and we all practically roll on the floor laughing."

Sam stared at him in wonder. "Wow, I wish I had a teacher like him."

"No problem. You'll have that teacher *himself* in two years, buddy."

———— ✸✸ ————

One evening Jacob listened to a speech Hitler was giving on the radio. He said the harsh anti-Semitic legislation of the 1935 *Nuremberg Laws* was an attempt to find a legal solution to the 'Jewish problem'.

Jacob cringed. The monster spoke directly to him. It chilled him to the core of his being. He understood every word because he studied German in school, and spoke it with German people around town.

If the laws failed, Hitler added, it would be necessary to *transfer the problem to the Nazi party for a final solution. If the Jews and their money practices got Germany into another war, the result would be their total annihilation.*

Jacob's scalp prickled. *Total annihilation?* His hands felt clammy. *What do Germans think when they hear 'transfer the problem to the Nazi party for a final solution'? Doesn't that bother them?*

He tried to sort out his fear. Exactly what was he going to lose? Property? His life? He had no idea, but he believed if Hitler ever turned his gaze on them, it wouldn't be good.

He wouldn't bring it up to Mama or Papa. He'd wait and see what happened, but the fear nagged at the back of his mind more often now. Were they going to lose this, their little piece of heaven, their home and their lifestyle?

———— ❧ ————

Life went on more or less as usual while the Eisenbachs waited for the day they could finally answer the big question. The one many people in Europe tried to ignore or rationalize away: *WILL HITLER COME HERE?*

Meanwhile, he enjoyed staying busy and productive. He was the repairman around the house. If a light bulb needed attention or there was a wiring problem, he was your man. If there was a difficult door lock he'd be down on his knees fixing it. And his rates were totally reasonable: *zero zloty* per hour.

Mama had a laundress who helped her; they boiled clothes and rubbed them on a wash board, steam rolling off the pieces like storm clouds. They cranked them through a wringer, stopping every now and then to stretch or rub their backs. Next they had to drag them upstairs to air out in the attic.

Whenever Jacob saw them breathing hard, pulling and bumping the heavy wet bundles up the stairs, he couldn't stand it. He put down what he was doing and rushed to their side.

One spring day when he was 14, he finished helping with the laundry and dried his hands on his shirt. He heard a knock at the door.

He answered it and saw a boy standing there with flowers.

"You want to see Fela?" he asked, knowing the answer already.

"Yes, if I may."

Well, he's handsome; I'll give him that. "I'm sorry; she's not home."

The boy frowned. "Do you know when she'll be back? I told her I was coming over."

"You know, Fela has so many friends. I can't keep track of everywhere she goes. You can try to call her. Do you have a phone?"

"No. I'll just talk with her later. Would you give her these from Aaron, please?"

Jacob politely took them. He put the flowers on Fela's desk and went in his room to do some school work. He put his pencil down a moment and thought about the ineffective attempts of these boys to date Fela. *She has a ton of male admirers. If I were him, I'd just go play ball. Who needs the aggravation?"*

Then he remembered how he didn't like to lose. *Maybe I would just go find her and bring her back with me. That guy isn't going to get anywhere leaving flowers and walking away,* he chuckled. *Another member of Fela's Fan Club.*

—— ∞∞ ——

At a wedding one evening, Jacob fidgeted in his seat, waiting to see the bride come to the front. He thought of another wedding when he was seven. It was a snowy New Year's Eve; the hall was decorated beautifully. There was an elegant orchestra and 300 people. People threw confetti up during the *Gladdening of the Bride* dance they performed around the young girl.

He wondered if this one would be as much fun. When the bride finally appeared, her dark hair was in little curls on top and an intricately embroidered satin veil flowed from them. Her snow-white dress had small, finely stitched roses on it. Papa loved the fabric and complimented her on the dress later during the reception.

The Rabbi performed the ceremony under the *chupah*. The couple looked nervous, clutching each other's hands. For good luck, the groom stomped on a glass wrapped in a napkin.

At last, the fun part; the traditional dancing. Jacob jumped up eagerly and participated in the rousing *Horah*. They entertained the bride and groom, who laughed and clapped along. Guests called out for a kiss, and the couple gave each other a chaste peck, to laughter and applause.

Finally, the bride and groom danced together. She had that dreamy look of love, and he had that nervous look of sudden responsibility.

After dinner, guests spent the evening dancing. If there was a good-looking Miss anywhere, Jacob would find her and ask her to dance. That was even more fun than throwing confetti around.

One year his class took a field trip to Warsaw on a super-speed train; they arrived in an hour, streaking through the countryside at 110 mph. It was the fastest train in Poland, sleek and shiny. The boys were thrilled; it felt like flying.

Jewish culture was rich with celebrations and social life; Jacob's family enjoyed their lives to the fullest. It was a good thing they did, because like that speeding train, they were rushing 110 miles per hour towards their destiny. They had no idea how terrible the end of that ride was going to be.

CHAPTER 6

All In The Family   1937

~∞∞∞~

Cousin Schmul, Mama's brother's son;
died in Auschwitz
(Dr. Eisenbach's collection)

COUSIN SCHMUL AND HIS APPETITE arrived about 6:30 one evening; Mama welcomed him to join the family for sandwiches. He was her brother's son; she was very close to her siblings and their children. She had four sisters and another brother, as well.

"Where's your little sister?" Jacob asked his cousin.

Schmul dragged his eyes away from the tempting food on the table. "She's home with my mother, dressing up in Mama's wedding dress and pearls."

"Where did she find a bridegroom this young?" Jacob dead-panned.

Schmul chuckled. "She won't have a problem, that one. She'll just grab him by the collar and take him to the rabbi." His eyes raced back to the food. "Am I the only visitor tonight?"

"Yes, you're our honored guest," Mama said. "Help yourself to some herring and pumpernickel." Soon they were lost in the delights of Schmaltz herring, the gold standard of all herring.

Before they could finish, Mama answered the door and found Lolek, another cousin, standing with his hands in his pockets and his hair askew from a sudden gust of wind. His father and Papa were brothers. She gave him a big, warm hug and invited him to share the feast.

Relatives came to visit all the time, sailing through the door with big hugs and hearty laughter. Jacob loved them all but was a typical boy. Sometimes he was annoyed to have to hug so many people hello and good-bye, especially the jolly aunts who squeezed too tightly. He was an active boy, always having some project calling for his attention.

No wonder they had lots of company; no one could cook like Mama. The soups she brewed on that old-fashioned stove were delicious beyond description, like chicken noodle and matzo ball. She was a world-class baker; the aroma floated down the street, cinnamon and butter, pecans and caramel, teasing the children's noses while they walked the last block home from school.

One evening he and his best friend Jack went to a movie and watched the accompanying newsreel. Hitler was making a speech, waving his fist around and pounding the podium. German women and girls were screaming and crying, swooning and love-sick.

"What a waste of female adoration," said Jack, always in the market for romance. They were walking home.

Jacob shook his head in disgust. "What is it about him? He's ugly as a mud fence and looks ridiculous with that little chopped-off mustache. I bet a lot of those people make fun of him behind his back."

"They should do it in front of him then?" Jack quipped.

"Not if they want to stay alive," said Jacob.

"I'll bet nobody dares say what they really think. Would you? I mean, what can you admire about a man who makes laws to persecute a whole race of people? They are just acting this way because he demands it."

"They like those Volkswagens, the Autobahn, the jobs and all that. They've sold their souls for it, Jack."

"How *Faustian* of them," his friend chuckled. "I heard they go on cruises the government pays for."

"Are you serious? Cruises?" Jacob hadn't heard this.

"Absolutely. Plus a lot of Germans have new Volkswagens, radios and even record players." A look of disgust settled on his face. "They didn't sell themselves cheaply."

"I guess *not*. I wonder about Hitler's plans for Jews. Remember that Nuremberg speech? He said he'd turn the 'Jewish problem' over to the Nazi party for a 'final solution'? Do you think he's moving towards that, whatever it is?"

"It's scary as hell, Kuba; I won't lie. I try not to dwell on it too much because he hasn't done anything to Poland yet. Maybe he won't. Maybe, God willing, he'll keep his hands to himself."

"Let that be from your mouth right up to God's ears; now let's forget Hitler for a while. It's a nauseating subject. Have you met any cute girls lately?" Jacob loved to hear the scoop.

"I met one at a wedding, a year older than me."

"*Now* you're talking. Tell me."

"She's pretty, but she hinted she has a boyfriend. I'm not like you because you would have already charmed her away from him."

"Very funny," said Jacob, "but don't stop. I like it."

Fela continued to have male admirers. Even Mama's cardiologist was in love with her. She was only 16 and that didn't bother him in the least. He made house calls and one day after seeing Mama he was hanging around, flirting with Fela.

"Jacob, come here, please." she called out.

He came into the room and looked at her, slightly annoyed at the disruption of his studies. She pulled him aside.

"Stay in the room with me as long as he's here" she whispered.

"Really?"

"Yes, Kuba, really. I don't trust him at all. He keeps leering at me and tries to get me to go out with him every time he comes over."

"Just let him try something," mumbled Jacob. No one was going to bother his sister. Unless she *wanted* him to, of course.

The cardiologist soon grew tired of Jacob sitting on the couch glaring at him. He excused himself and left the house. Fela and Jacob laughed and shook hands.

"You like Max well enough, don't you?" Jacob asked, referring to the man who often took her out to the finest restaurants. "I can get rid of him for you and you'll be rid of two guys for the price of one."

"Oh, no. Max is a sweetheart. I don't have to worry with him."

"Well, I'm glad to hear it," said Jacob, all puffed up. When Papa was at the factory he relished the opportunity to be man of the house.

He loved to tease his older sister. "Remind me how you met him. Didn't you find him over at the homeless mission?"

"That's cute, Kuba. Cousin Marysia introduced us. He's a pharmacist like she is."

"Is there any place you can go without men trying to worm their way into your life? How about at Temple?"

"Silly," she laughed, as she walked away. "Go back to your home-work." Then she turned back and said "By the way, you said *two for the price of one*. What is your price?"

"Make me *paczki* or *sernik* one day."

"You dream big, Kuba. Like I could bake filled donuts or cheesecake!"

"Well, spend less time on the phone and have Mama teach you how." She made a face at him and waved him off. "Thanks for your help, Kuba."

Over the next few weeks Jacob continued to feel uneasy. Hitler had already taken some action with German Jews. Nazis dumped a whole group of them on the Polish border and said "Get out" after taking all their possessions; this had included the Steins. All of these 'deportees' were now homeless.

He thought about that warning 'Jews will be *totally annihilated*' and wondered why Hitler didn't say '*the country we defeat will be totally annihilated*'? Why just the Jews? How was killing Jews going to help him become powerful in Europe? Jews were only a minority of the population. He couldn't understand racial hatred of any type, but especially not this extreme.

There had to be *somebody* in a position to make a difference who could help. He would give it some thought and maybe come up with a new angle. If so, he'd discuss it with his teacher.

He knew many fine minds had toyed with this question, and he also knew there *had to be* a logical solution. Everything in life succumbed to logic and scientific laws. Sooner or later *someone* was going to find a way to stop the monster that sported that ridiculous mustache.

Henry approached Jacob after supper. "Hey, I'm building a super bridge. Want to help me with it?"

"I'm sorry, buddy, I have some thinking to do."

"Thinking? Man, you're just no fun anymore," Henry complained. He shook his head. "*Thinking!* Sam, will you help? That's if you don't have to *think* tonight?"

Jacob ignored him; his mind was on bigger things.

Sam nodded and followed Henry to the other room. Henry was a handful sometimes, but Sam was an easy-going kid and would go along.

Jacob went to his room to do his thinking. He wrote down some ideas and wrinkled up the paper. He didn't have any more answers than anybody else. And Papa didn't have any ideas, either. *Frustration. Fear. Anger.* His companions too often now.

Jews were concerned, but not aware they were in such great peril; everyone intellectualized the possibilities of this and that, but nobody *did* anything. Sadly, not just for young Henry, but for *all of them*, the fun was nearly over. They would only enjoy their lives for a little longer. The madness was inching its way closer and closer every day.

CHAPTER 7

Living In The Shadow Of Hitler   1937-1938

—∞∞∞—

(2) Hitler, Goebbels and Goebbel's daughter, Helga Susanne. Hitler liked children and often held her on his lap during meetings. She paid for her daddy's politics with her life.

PEOPLE IN EUROPE WERE NERVOUS as frightened rabbits; the 1930's were coming to a close and the situation was deteriorating as Hitler turned his greedy eyes toward Austria and Czechoslovakia. Soon they would be his. The USA, who had the ability to bring some real power to the cause, was refusing to get involved. The Great War, WWI, was enough for them.

Cleaning his room one weekend, Jacob came across his picture of Iron Leg. He set it up on the chest of drawers next to Mama's picture.

Too bad Hitler couldn't have played soccer with Iron Leg. One good kick and the world wouldn't have had to worry about Nazi Germany. Jacob smiled. *What a pleasant thought.*

He pulled out his military uniform and brushed it off. At school he was in a required class to introduce students to the military way of doing things.

He enjoyed the class; he particularly liked it when they saw an officer on the street with two or three stars on his hat. They would salute him and he would salute them back; they almost burst their uniform buttons with pride.

He was thankful he didn't have to learn how to operate heavy artillery, or the finer points of killing people. German youths were forced to join Hitler Youth and Hitler Maidens where they were swamped with Nazi rules, plans, war techniques and Nazi philosophy. Jacob was content with the academic version of the military; he certainly didn't want to get involved with actually *doing* it, unless there was no other choice.

Those poor kids had to dedicate their lives to Adolf and swear allegiance until death. He really had them in his grip. They marched around like a bunch of little Hitlers, all steely-eyed with determination. Jacob watched the newsreels and couldn't imagine being part of that.

Papa poked his head in the door. "How is the room coming? I was hoping we could play some chess."

"I won't be long. Say, Papa, what do you think about the kids in Germany? I heard they turn their parents in if they criticize Hitler."

"I don't know what to believe, Kuba. I read something about it in the paper. I'm more concerned about violence against Jews right here at home."

"The *pogroms?*"

"Yes. Do you use caution now when you go anywhere?"

"Sure, Papa, don't worry. You can set up the chessboard. I'll be done here in a minute."

Papa nodded and left the room. Jacob was skilled at chess and was a good challenge for Papa.

"Ready?" he asked when Jacob emerged from his room.

"My *middle name* is '*Ready*'."

Papa laughed. "White or black?"

"I'll take black. I'll be the bad guy."

They began to play, attempting to carefully consider their moves while discussing Hitler, quite a juggling act.

"Abuse of Jews is not going to stop, is it Papa?"

"Probably not. It's been happening since ancient times."

"What keeps it going?"

"Political, racial and religious beliefs. Right now it's inflamed by Hitler. You know how he says Jews are supporting *communism?*"

Jacob moved his pawn while saying "That's ridiculous. Who would want the government to take all your stuff?"

"Exactly; it makes no sense. We are business people," Papa said, moving a rook forward two spaces. "Hitler plays that tune for his people on a concert violin. *'Jews want communism, it advances their financial interest. Jews want a war.'* All lies. Much of it thanks to Propaganda Minister Goebbels. I think he should be called the minster of something else; something cows leave behind."

Jacob chuckled. "Whatever they say, no one is getting any of *our* stuff; I don't care if the communists set up tents outside our apartment." He moved another pawn.

Papa laughed. "I don't think you have to worry about that, Kuba."

"What if Hitler comes over here? What do we do?"

"What would he want with us? It's not like we are loaded with oil wells. In Germany, the common people drive Volkswagens. Here, most of us are unable to afford any kind of car."

"Maybe he wants to come here and provide us all with Volkswagens," joked Jacob, moving his knight.

Papa grimaced. "Don't even joke about him coming here. Hopefully it will never happen; he has plenty to deal with in Germany. He's had a long struggle for control over other political parties and he still has huge economic problems."

"He does? The newsreels certainly don't show *that*."

"Your move, Kuba."

"Okay, here." He moved a bishop. "So what about Hitler?"

"Everyone hopes to keep him happy with trade agreements and certain concessions he wants. The United States won't get involved, so we're on our own. We just have to pray it doesn't happen."

"But what if it does?"

Papa sighed and looked at him. "Don't borrow trouble, Son. If it happens, we'll deal with it. Please don't worry your brothers or Mama."

Don't borrow trouble? That was a non-answer, and Jacob was frightened. "Do you think we should leave the country?"

"No, I'd have to sell the factory; start all over."

Jacob remembered the game and captured one of Papa's pawns. He watched Papa take the pawn off the board and studied his father's hands. So strong and protective, like his personality. *He must be the best father in the world.*

Papa asked. "How would you feel about moving away and losing everything?"

"I'd hate it. He could come here and take everything away from us if we stayed here, though, couldn't he? We're like these weak little pawns, while Hitler is the queen. We can make one step forward, but he's so powerful he can maneuver all over the board."

"Interesting analogy, Kuba, but you are getting way ahead of yourself. He has not yet made a military move, and he may not if people give him enough concessions." He moved a knight.

"Should I join the army when I'm old enough? Not that I want to do that."

"I'd rather you completed your education in dentistry. I was never in the army; I'm not inclined to fighting."

"Sometimes at school we think we're something special in our military uniforms."

"I know. Just remember, Kuba, lots of people die in those uniforms."
Jacob's face grew cold. The familiar fear was back, running up and down his spine. *Lots of people die. Well, lots of people die every day nowadays, whatever they are doing. Like those people in the park.* Suddenly he felt light-headed.

Papa noticed. "I wouldn't worry too much. Don't forget what you've seen and heard is propaganda. *Lies.* People have been starving over there; their money became worthless. Not too long ago they had to pay a *billion* marks for a loaf of bread."

"A *billion marks for bread?*" Jacob's jaw dropped.

"Yes. They actually took their paper money to the store in wheelbarrows to buy that loaf of bread."

"That's unbelievable." Jacob moved his queen over to protect the king, his concentration on the game rapidly deteriorating.

"Yes, it is. So you see he's got a lot to do there."

"So we should just not worry about Hitler?"

"I wouldn't say *totally relax,* but stay alert and think positively," Papa said, as he neatly captured Jacob's queen with his rook. "I believe we have checkmate."

"I believe in being positive, too." He looked at the board. "Right now I'm positively losing this game," he laughed. "I give up; good job, Papa."

———

One evening during that fearful time Jacob went to chat with Mama in her room. This thing with the German children was still bothering him.

If Hitler is crazy enough to get children to report their parents, thus orphaning themselves, he obviously has a screw loose and God knows what he'll do. Meanwhile they have to pledge their own lives to Hitler, for God's sake.

Mama was sitting at her dressing table, brushing her hair. "Have you heard that German kids turn their parents in if they criticize Hitler or the Nazis?"

"I don't believe it, Kuba. I think it's all a lie."

"I hope so. Why would they want to have their parents imprisoned or shot?"

Mama started to pale; she put the brush down.

Oh, no. Jacob wished he could eat his words. He'd worried her again, just what he vowed not to do.

He quickly backpedaled. "I didn't mean to upset you Mama, I was just curious, that's all." He pasted a smile on his face.

"Some people are trying to rile everyone up to have a war. I don't listen. I'd rather have peace of mind," she said.

Jacob danced around the subject a little more. "You're right, Mama. Kids wouldn't do that. It's ridiculous, they would be orphans."

She smiled at him in agreement and returned to brushing her hair.

Jacob left the room, his collar suddenly too tight. He swore not to repeat that mistake. She wasn't strong enough for this. And he *definitely* wasn't going to continue talking about Hitler with Papa, who sometimes gave him too much information and scared him. Probably because he was the oldest.

He was proud that Papa thought he could handle it, though. Just thinking about that made him lift his chin and stand a little prouder.

In spite of having grown up in a candy store, Papa doesn't sugar coat anything, he thought with a wry smile. *That's a good one, I'll have to share it with Jack.*

The next evening, Jacob hurried to finish filling some cigarette papers with tobacco for Papa. Jack was coming over for a bite to eat.

He would talk with him about his worries. Nazi propaganda made Hitler look so powerful. And the bigwig Nazis were always in the paper. He'd rather not have soiled his eyes looking at any of them.

"Kuba!" Jack said when he arrived. They grabbed a sandwich and some cookies from the kitchen and went to Jacob's room.

"I have a question for you, Jack. How could Hitler do anything to us without an army? According to the Versailles Treaty, he can only have a limited army."

"Right. I have a sneaking suspicion he's not above preparing for war anyway. Do you really think he's a good little boy and follows instructions?"

"No, I don't," Jacob admitted. "Hitler building up a secret army. That's a comforting thing to ponder on a lazy afternoon in the park."

"Yes, isn't it?" replied Jack.

"If it's going to come to that, why don't we get our families together and leave Poland? You are always talking about Switzerland. I hear they have such a peaceful and prosperous country," Jacob said.

"I would love nothing better. Let's keep that in mind. All we have to do is convince our families."

"I know," said Jacob, losing his smile. "Papa doesn't want to leave his factory, and I can't blame him. But if our *lives* are at stake, maybe he'll reconsider."

School went on as if there were no Hitler looming over them. In high school, they were required to buy a season ticket to the theater. Most of the teenage boys had other ideas of a good time; they certainly didn't push people aside to get through the entrance.

Jacob followed a school acquaintance, Abe, up the steps of the balcony. "Did you find them?" he asked about their seats.

"Not yet. I figure about twelve more rows," Abe said. They climbed the steps. "Here."

"The nosebleed section, wouldn't you know."

"Don't worry, Kuba; we'll be able to hear everything. Probably more than we want to."

Once settled in, the project started to become more enjoyable. They sat back and relaxed in the cushy seats, tycoons of the theater. "*This* is the way to study, eh, Kuba?"

"Yeah, it *is* fun, though not a very *manly* activity," he chuckled.

"Hey, speak for yourself. I watch plays in a *very* manly way," quipped Abe.

After the play their task was to discuss it and write an opinion. Jacob was a science-minded guy, but he loved this assignment.

Fela went to an all-Jewish high school for girls. She was very bright; her girlfriend and she taught themselves how to read *backwards*. They also could speak that way.

"*madA si yllaer etuc*," she'd say. Her friend would answer, "*oD uoy kniht eh sekil uoy?*"

They often carried on conversations no one else could understand. Jacob would just shake his head. *Girls. What will they think of next?*

In *Ignacy Skorupki* High School where Jacob went, the first challenge was getting used to it being a half-Catholic and half-Jewish school; he loved it. It was a boys' school in a large, dignified building named after a priest, a Polish national hero. The students were good kids. Though Jacob was not large in stature, he was never bullied and had many friends. His school was very important to him.

Poland provided an outstanding education. Trade schools were one option, but those who chose high school were prepared to go to *graduate* school afterwards, such as law, engineering, medical or dental school.

One day after the midday meal, there was a loud banging on the front door. Startled, Jacob opened it cautiously.

"Hey, old man, why are you banging on the door? Is everything okay?" Jacob asked when he saw Jack, standing there with a broad grin.

"Good. Better than good. I have some juicy news for you."

Jacob wondered what young man or teenage couple Jack was going to gossip about. He took him back into his room and said "Tell me."

"My uncle's neighbor just got back from a business trip to Germany."

"How is he able to get into Germany? And why would he even *want to?*"

"He's not Jewish, so they let him in. He has some connection over there, maybe a relative, who gives him pictures or information. I don't know how the source gets the info, but he does." Jack chuckled, "It's a steady stream of it."

"Hmm. Maybe he's a spy. Is it dangerous for you to tell me this?" Jacob looked over his shoulder out the window.

"No cloak and dagger," laughed Jack. "His friend is not a spy. He's an engineer and deals with their automotive production, maybe sells them things, I don't know. I do know it is getting harder and harder for him to get into Germany. You'd think they would want the business."

"True. So what's your news?"

"You know those bride schools?"

"No."

"You don't? Well, Creepy Goebbels has designed bride schools to teach young girls how to be perfect Nazi wives for the elite SS officers."

"Heinrich Himmler's thugs. So tell me." Jacob leaned forward, anxious to hear the juicy part.

"Goebbels, with his sparkling personality and good looks" – both boys chortled over that – "was seen sneaking around the Bride School gardens at night looking in the windows."

"Really?" Jacob's eyebrows went straight up. The jerk looked like a mouse to him; Goebbels was no handsome ladies' man, though after the war they would learn he had kept a mistress.

"Yes, he said he was hoping to see them dancing."

"Oh, right!" scoffed Jacob. "Dancing." They almost burst with glee at the ridiculous idea.

"So, there was an Intelligence Department report on it. That's what my uncle's neighbor found out."

"Wow, he really has some good contacts." Jacob was wide-eyed, imagining doing business in Nazi Germany, a frightening thought. "Did Goebbels get in trouble?"

"Are you kidding? Has anyone replaced him? No, Goebbels is one of Hitler's golden boys. Hitler's own Intelligence Department probably didn't have the guts to tell him. Lucky for Goebbels because with his club foot he would have a hard time running away."

They leaned back in their chairs laughing again at how Nazis were such idiots. "Too bad they couldn't accidentally blow themselves up sometime. And Hitler right in there with them." his friend said.

"No kidding. By the way, do you ever get scared he'll come over here?"

"Hitler or Goebbels?"

"Hitler, you *dummkopf*," Jacob said, showing off a little German.

"What would he want with us? We don't have tons of wealth. We're just plain folks here with modest homes. We aren't loaded with gold or oil, either."

"You sound just like my father. He doesn't think I should worry, but maybe he's wishful thinking."

"If he is, Kuba, I'm right there with him, hoping Hitler keeps his filthy hands to himself."

Even while the boys spoke these words, the eve of the madness was upon them.

CHAPTER 8

The Eve of the Madness   1938 – 1939

(3) Goebbels and his children at a Nazi Christmas party, 1937.
A proud father, he never seemed bothered about the Nazis
murdering children.

TALK WAS EVERYWHERE ABOUT HITLER'S intention to annihilate Jews;
many Jews scoffed at it. Some thought the rumor-spreader was crazy.
"Just the ranting of a sick brain," they would reassure each other. The
more educated and upper-class Jews in Germany felt less vulnerable,
but to their horror they would discover they were wrong – *dead* wrong.

Jacob and Jack were discussing Hitler again while walking home from high school.

"What are you going to do if Hitler starts sending his goons over here?"

"If it comes to that I'll come find you or you come to me. Our families can stay together. There is safety in numbers, Kuba."

"I can't talk with my mother because she isn't well, and my father rationalizes about it. I'm glad I can talk with you."

"I accept I-O-U's or cash."

Jacob chuckled. Jack Sieradski, best friend, medicine for the soul.

In newsreels they saw what Germany allowed the world to see: the ceremonial hoop-la, parades, speeches, and rallies. Goebbels designed it all and even made films, including his *Titanic,* where he used a bit of Nazi artistic license. It featured German heroes and selfish, bumbling Englishmen.

He had flashes of genius. For the election of 1932 he had Hitler campaigning from city to city by *airplane*; no one had done that before. In splashy productions with flag waving, music and fiery speeches, Nazis totally awed people. Soldiers marched smartly down the street with torches that lit up the night. Germans rushed forward to follow them and hysteria carried the evening. The German people appeared to be under some kind of dark spell.

"Hitler has a kind of charisma that just *enraptures* Germans, especially those ice-blue eyes that just *nail* people, but Goebbels? No physical appeal whatever," Jacob said. "Yet they get almost as crazy when he talks, according to the newsreels."

"I don't get the appeal of either of them; Hitler looks like a sad old man to me."

"Maybe he has a guilty conscience," Jacob said. 'Is that even possible?"

"In science fiction, maybe, but not in this word," chuckled Jack.

Then Jacob thought about the Fuhrer's planned victims. Nothing funny about that. It sent a shiver down Jacob's spine. "Let's get off this subject; go outside and knock a ball around."

The following evening Mama was drying dishes when she and Papa came into the living room. She rubbed at a spot on a glass. "I can't believe what's going on. We have to stay close to God in these times."

"Why? What happened?" Jacob was alarmed.

She put down the glass and covered her eyes. She wasn't feeling well.

"She's talking about all the hostility to Jews." Papa looked at Mama. "This is nothing new, Dear. Don't be so worried. We'll be all right, and go on as we always have."

Jacob could see fear in Papa's eyes. They knew something.

Papa gently took Mama's arm. "Here, come sit down with me, Sara. Jacob, can you finish up the dishes?"

"Sure, Papa" he replied, wishing he could be alone with Papa to ask him.

Later Jacob found him reading in his bedroom and seized the opportunity.

"It's not much," Papa said. "Her friend has a son in the army; she heard that our government is very nervous for Jewish soldiers. They replaced their ID tags to hide their Jewish identity. Just in case of capture."

A small roar, on its way to being huge, filled Jacob's ears. "That sounds pretty serious to me. Our government must expect war."

"Now, don't borrow trouble, Kuba. They say it's just a precaution. Jews are mistreated in the army. Maybe this means they're getting a little more respect."

They were interrupted when Mama called her children together in the living room.

"Come in here, Fela, Sam and Henry" she called out. She glanced in the bedroom. Jacob, you too."

They came into the living room with puzzled faces and worried eyes.

"Are you alright?" Sam asked, pale and tense.

"I'm fine. Come closer to me." They went up to her and she put her arms around all of them at once. The three older ones looked at her, studying her face for a clue. Henry was fiddling with a toy car. "You are my most precious possessions," she said, as she often did. "Hitler can have anything of mine except you."

"What about Papa?" Henry looked up, saucer-eyed.

"Don't worry; Hitler can't have him, either. I love him, too," she laughed. "All of you."

Jacob silently prayed for God to keep her well. He didn't like to see his parents anxious. The very foundation of his life was slipping out from under him.

Living next door to Hitler didn't make for an easy night's sleep, especially when Hitler claimed part of Austria and started flexing his military muscles. However, Austrians practically threw themselves into his arms during the 1938 *Anshluss* takeover. Hitler's ridiculous reason was people of German descent lived in the area. Actually, *Herr Hitler* didn't really *need* a reason to do crazy things. He just did them.

Papa threw down the newspaper in disgust one evening. "People keep hoping Hitler can be appeased with trade agreements and such. Now he wants part of Czechoslovakia. Those idiots in France and Britain want to give it to him; persuade the Czechs to give in."

"Why does he only want part of Czechoslovakia?"

"Well, Kuba, I guess Germans are living in that area, just as they were in Austria. Unbelievable. There are Germans in the United States; does he want that, too?"

Jacob was horrified. "Why would France and Britain help Hitler? What's the matter with them?"

"They don't want war so they are constantly kissing his feet. They'll want it soon enough when he shows up at their borders." Papa lit a cigarette that Jacob had lovingly crafted for him the night before.

Jacob watched him concentrate on lighting it and throw the match into an ashtray. When Papa closed his eyes and inhaled the smoke, Jack studied his worry-worn face. If only he could *do something to ease the burden on his parents.*

"Papa, the army changing the religion of Jews on their ID's must mean something. Do they know something they aren't telling us?"

"Kuba, sometimes I don't know what to think anymore. The situation is starting to feel unstable and frightening."

Once again, Jacob wished he hadn't asked.

A week later, Mama was in no condition to worry about Hitler. More and more she lay in bed with poor circulation.

Jacob passed by the bedroom and his heart broke every time he saw her lying there, struggling for life. More often, he sang to her now.

One overcast spring day, Fela was with her. She screamed "Jacob! Mama is bleeding from her mouth. Get the doctor right away! Hurry!"

His fumbling fingers struggled with the dial; finally he heard it ringing. No answer. He kept trying but couldn't get through. He paced around with the receiver, trying a few more times. He threw the phone down.

"I'm going down there. I can't reach him."

He ran out the door and down the steps to the street. His feet couldn't move fast enough; the doctor lived a mere block away, but he felt like he was running under water. When he got there, puffing like a steam engine, he could barely speak. Finally he got some breath and yelled "Help us! Mama's bleeding."

They immediately returned in the doctor's car, with Jacob trying to staunch his panic, one hand on the dashboard, one on the door handle. When they arrived, they found the family in tears around Mama's bed. The doctor examined her and sadly shook his head.

"I'm sorry. She's in heaven. She was already gone when I got here."

"No!" screamed Fela, collapsing in Papa's arms. "I saw her go to sleep, but I didn't know she was dying."

The wind was knocked right out of Jacob. He wasn't with her when she died. He couldn't bear to see her like that. He went to his room and wept, then he stopped himself. He didn't need to feel so guilty; it was understandable that he had been gone. He was getting the doctor. And she knew how much he loved her. He studied her picture on the chest of drawers. That wonderful, loving face. He was glad he'd shown his love all the time by doing things like giving up soccer to sing for her.

Per Jewish tradition, they had a beautiful funeral for her the next day. Half the students of Jacob's high school attended. He stared at the coffin, struggling with the fact that he would never lay eyes on her again. They were going to have to learn to live without her. *How* they would do that, he had no idea; she was the center of the family.

———— ✐ ————

Jacob's suspicions were correct. Germany was better off and stronger than people thought. The economic growth of Germany was finally acknowledged internationally and called the 'German Miracle'. *Time Magazine* said for better or worse Hitler had most influenced events of 1938.

"Have you heard?" Papa said as he walked in the door one evening early in 1939, in a cloud of fury, his voice strained and tight. "*Time Magazine* named Hitler 1938 *Man of the Year.* What is *wrong* with the world?"

"Oh, Papa. That's terrible. Now he will be all full of himself and get worse," Jacob worried. He stared at the radio, where the news was announcing an upcoming story about it.

"I'm afraid of that, too." Papa looked grim. "We don't need to be praising him. That's just adding gasoline to his fire."

"What fire?" asked 11-year-old Henry, who was passing through.

"That's just a term that means Hitler's burning desire to accomplish things," Jacob explained.

Henry gazed out the window, like Hitler's burning desire might be outside.

With that, Papa left the room. Jacob stared hard at the radio, willing it to give him a better answer. This had to be a hoax. Surely *Time Magazine* was more enlightened than *that*.

But the radio made it plain it was no hoax. Hitler was named *Man of the Year* because, among other things, he took part of Czechoslovakia with no bloodshed and turned it into a peaceful puppet government. Britain's Prime Minister Chamberlain helped negotiate the annexation to keep Adolf happy. The Czechs themselves had little say in it.

Jacob wanted to thump the radio. *What will become of us if the American magazine is calling a Jew-hater Man of the Year? Will America be buddies with him now?* It seemed anything was possible these terrible days.

August, 1939: the very eve of the madness. In a few days, Hitler would make his move and horrify the world.

CHAPTER 9

The Terror Begins   1939 – 1940

*(4) The Nazis occupy Jacob's home town of Łódź September, 1939.
Horrified, he and his family watched this appalling display.*

THE WOLF WAS UPON THEM. September 1, 1939 Jacob woke up to the jarring sound of bombs exploding.

At 4:45 in the morning Nazi General Johannes Blaskowitz's 8th Army began the campaign against Łódź on the ground, while Nazi airplanes dropped bombs. Explosions shook the ground and rattled windows. Jacob and the family raced to the windows but could not see any smoke or fire; they knew it was *somewhere* in their city.

"Papa! We have to get out of here!" cried Sam, clinging to him.

"I'm sorry, Son. There's nowhere to go. They must be concentrating on the other side of town. Maybe they will stay over there; our city is huge."

Papa was putting on a brave show for his children. No one ever knew what Hitler might do next. The second-to-second insecurity was crushing; Jews could never relax.

Sam went over and put his arm around Fela, standing there in her nightgown. Henry was hiding behind her and peeking out at the windows. "I miss Mama," Sam cried, big tears rolling down his cheeks. He was fourteen, but sometimes he just needed his mother.

"Me, too," said Henry, now in tears as well. Fela put her arms around them. "I miss her too, but you know what? She is here with us. Right, Papa?"

"What?" He was scanning the skies.

"Mama is here with us."

"Oh. Yes, I think so." Papa wasn't really listening. That worried Jacob; usually anything about Mama got his attention. This must be frightening him badly. Jacob started to pace around the living room. *Those bloodsucking MONSTERS.*

On the radio Hitler had recently said *Bombs are going to fly over your city.* Jacob tried to ignore it as so much bluster, but obviously Hitler had been completely serious.

"What's going to happen?" he asked Papa for the hundred-and-tenth time.

"We'll be all right, Kuba. God is on our side, not Hitler's."

There was no arguing that point. If God was on your side, who could defeat you? There was no way God could *possibly* be on Hitler's side; of *that* he was certain.

"Feel better?" Papa asked.

"I guess so, but still. You know, God took Mama. I prayed that He wouldn't do that."

"We don't understand the way God works, Kuba. Maybe He wanted her to be spared this."

"Maybe," Jacob said as he took his place next to him at the window, feeling a huge empty place in his heart from the loss of Mama. Papa put his arm around him.

They watched on and off throughout the bombing, which never came close to them. They stayed indoors, so they couldn't really hear everything, but they had a pretty good idea what was happening.

Polish General Juliusz Rómmel's Łódź army courageously tried to defend the city against the initial German attacks. Frightened and confused, the army pretty much rolled over like puppies. After all, it was that or be slaughtered – they had nothing worthy of the name *defense* to use against the *Blitzkrieg*.

After the bombing, there was an eerie quiet. More bombing happened the next day. A few days later Jacob and his family watched with horror as Nazi soldiers marched in step down the street in front of their apartment. His worst nightmare was unfolding right in front of him. People were scurrying off the streets to get out of the way.

After the victory parade, some Nazi soldiers remained to stand guard on the streets. They had killed all leaders, Jewish or not, so there would be no revolt. Over six days they spread out and occupied the whole city.

People were stupefied, staring at one atrocity after another. Jews were forced to clear out of their workplaces. German soldiers were barking orders at them and if they didn't cooperate, Nazis had no problem with murder. No aggression was too vile for them, including bashing babies against brick walls.

Non-Jewish people were also victims if they resisted Nazi occupation. No one knew it yet, but Hitler's goal was to clear out the Poles. The Slavic race was inferior in his opinion; then he would have more land for Germany. Meanwhile Nazis plundered stores and factories.

Here and there tall soldiers in black uniforms with skull and cross-bones on their hats and lapels stood in groups. These were the SS, Heinrich Himmler's elite group of assassins whose girlfriends attended the bride schools.[2] People couldn't take their eyes off them; they were like ugly, poisonous spiders, fascinating but deadly.

Hitler now had Łódź in his back pocket. Jews finally had their answer to the question *Is Hitler coming here?* It was small comfort that they didn't have to wonder anymore. They needed to get far, far away from this. But where could Jacob's family go? Just leave Papa's business behind? Was it too late to go, anyway?

Many Jews were fleeing to a little town twenty miles east, bringing their belongings in carts. Their children with smudged little faces followed closely, carrying a doll or a teddy bear. People in business attire walked along with those in peasant clothes. They went down the streets heading for the road out of town. There was no sound of Polish laughter that day.

Cherished family pictures were tied on top of some of the bundles. Most of the people in those pictures, if alive, wouldn't be for long. Still in shock, Jacob and his family watched the sad migration of people flow down the street outside their apartment.

"We might as well just stay here," said Papa. "If they want to kill us, they'll do it no matter where we go."

Jacob could hardly believe what he was hearing. He waited till the younger ones were in other rooms, then asked "You just want to give in? That's our only option? Stay here and hope they don't kill us?"

"I'm sorry, Kuba, we have no other choice. I am not going to have us run off like a bunch of mice and just give them everything. I'd rather stay here and stand our ground. If they want to kill all the Jews, it's not hard to go twenty miles over there and kill them."

Jacob was speechless, unusual for him.

---

2 *United States Holocaust Memorial Museum. "The Holocaust." Holocaust Encyclopedia. http://www.ushmm.org/wlc/en/article.php?ModuleId=10005143*

Papa continued. "If we leave, Nazis will take over our home. I am not willing to live in the streets. I'll take the risk that they will be satisfied with having conquered the area so they can control things to their advantage."

Jacob rarely disagreed with his father, but he wasn't sure what to do. Of course he would cooperate, but he would watch the situation carefully. It if changed, he might be able to persuade Papa to leave Poland.

Next day Jacob heard the stories that left no question what Nazis were about: pure evil. They called themselves *children of the gods. What* gods, people could only wonder.

On a road just outside of town, the *children of the gods* fired on the migrating Jews, including children, with machine guns. Bodies littered the road.

He called his friend Jack frequently with no answer. He was becoming frantic by the time he reached him, and his friend told him about the scene on the road as he had observed it.

"We were thinking of leaving. We walked over to the area where people were flooding the road out of town, to have a look. I was going to call you to join us if it looked like a good plan."

"I guess it didn't, then."

"Absolutely not. When the soldiers came, guns in hand, we backed away. We didn't have luggage and weren't walking with those other people so they left us alone. Mothers and children were wounded and screaming, crawling over to the side of the road. Abe was running around with a bloody eye socket."

"Oh, my God," gasped Jacob. Ábe who?"

"The one from literature class."

Jacob swallowed hard. *The one I attended the play with.*

Jack continued. "Another boy was sprawled out in the road next to his baby sister. Bodies were piled up on each other. There were overturned carts, some crushing victims underneath." Jack was almost panting with anxiety.

"Are you all right?" asked Jacob, straining to stuff down his own panic.

"We're all okay. I can't believe it, Kuba. All those people killed on that road. Our fiends. They shot at them with *airplane fire*. Can you imagine running from *airplane fire*?"

"Murdering bastards," Jacob answered with all the venom he felt.

"Are you guys okay?" Jack asked. Are you going to stay?"

"We're all right and Papa wants to try to remain here. What about you?"

"Same here. I don't know if we should, though. I've seen some awful things, Kuba."

"There's more?"

"Much more. People have been beating Jews in the streets, robbing them and seizing their property."

"Which people?"

"Well, I don't have names, but they appeared to be Polish anti-Semites; Nazi soldiers were grabbing property, too."

"I can't believe what I'm hearing."

"I know; and Kuba?"

"Yes?"

"I can't believe we used to laugh about the Nazis."

"Me neither. Nothing funny about those demons from hell. You be careful, Jack, and call me tomorrow."

Jacob already had such horrible mental images, he was glad he hadn't been there to see anything further. *Airplane fire.* He could hardly believe human beings could do that. He would learn he lost many friends on that road.

Jacob was a sound sleeper most of the time, but that night it was impossible. He got up to get some milk; that was supposed to help.

Papa was up; he hadn't been to bed yet. He had a drink of something in his hand, sitting and staring. Papa didn't drink much, but this was bad. Very bad. He sipped at his drink, gazing at his son over the rim of his glass, as if words failed him.

"Papa, what will happen to us?" He repeated the well-worn question.

"We'll be strong and somehow survive." He had a faraway look, though, and mumbled that if Jews just kept to themselves and followed the rules, Hitler might leave them alone. Jacob felt uneasy; Papa seemed somewhere else.

Maybe he was getting tired of being asked the same questions over and over. Jacob resolved to be tougher. Papa probably needed some reassurance, too.

"Maybe the worst is over now, Papa."

"Who knows? I think the devil owns Hitler's mind and his soul."

"But *God* owns *our* minds and souls. We'll be all right."

"I hope so," said Papa.

Jacob headed for his bedroom. On the way, he looked in on Henry and Sam. Henry was snoozing away, a blanket pulled up to his chin. He was grateful Henry was calm enough to trust Papa and go to sleep. Sam was sitting up in bed, hugging his knees.

"It'll be okay, Sam. We're all fine now."

Sam nodded his head, but his eyes were huge.

"Just go to sleep and don't worry. Papa and I are handling things."

"You are? How?"

"He's going to talk to the – whoever is in charge – and find out what the rules are. We'll just do what they ask and we don't expect them to harass us after that. They have what they wanted. The city has surrendered and Hitler can take whatever he wants."

"What if he wants to kill us? Didn't he already kill a bunch of Jews?"

That was true. Jacob tried to smooth it out for Sam. "Well, he's done with that now; when they conquer a land, they take what they want and leave the people alone as long as they don't make trouble," he said, making it up as he went along.

"Good," said Sam, who pulled up the blanket and turned to his side. Jacob quietly closed the door and went to check on Papa once more. Though he was outwardly calm, Jacob was scared to death. He hoped Hitler was done with them now that he'd attacked their city and stolen so much.

Papa was sitting at the table, clutching his glass and staring at the floor as if in a stupor. Jacob tenderly took the glass from his hand and helped him stand up and walk toward the bedroom.

Unfortunately Hitler was far from through with them. The next day they wanted everyone out of their homes so they could plunder them.

Papa was standing with his children on the sidewalk in front of their apartment. He shook his head mournfully.

"You shouldn't have to see this. You've barely tasted life; you should be attending soccer games and going to the movies." Papa began to tremble. Jacob worried he would have a breakdown.

"I can deal with it, Papa. Don't worry," he said. "I am second in command around here, right? I'm 16 years old, and almost grown up."

That brought a chuckle from Papa.

"Sam and Henry are just children, only 12 and 14. I'll help you look after them."

Papa smiled at him. "And Fela? Are you going to take care of her, too?"

"No, she's 18. Practically an old lady."

"I am not," she said.

They laughed for the first time in days.

"You'll probably marry soon, Fela." Jacob said. "You must have a dozen guys who want to be with you." He was so proud of his beautiful, intelligent sister.

The soldiers were getting ready to enter Jacob's apartment building.

"Step back," said Papa. "Keep your eyes down. Don't make eye contact with them so they don't feel threatened. Just keep looking at the ground until I tell you to stop."

The children all did as they were told, Fela almost frightened into unconsciousness, Henry and Sam trembling and Jacob boiling with rage. Papa stood protectively in front of Fela. Jacob joined him.

Just let them try to touch her. He knew he was defenseless, but it made him feel better to *think tough.*

The *children of the gods* ransacked their home. To Papa's and Jacob's relief they left Fela alone. They wanted money, not pleasure.

Besides, Hitler had banned sex between Jews and Germans. Then he thought *Hitler's not here, so who knows what's holding them back? Maybe the soldiers are just too greedy for material things.*

They took everything they wanted including furniture and linens, and sent it all home to their families.

Jacob risked taking a peek at what they were doing. He smoldered as he watched one of them come outside, fondling Jacob's watch with dirty hands; he then pocketed it. A *Bar Mitzvah* gift from Papa when Jacob was 13, he treasured it.

When they were allowed back in their home, it was all torn up. Drawers were emptied, furniture missing, the closets rifled through. Even the bed linens were gone. Papa stared dully at the awful sight.

"Papa, it will be all right," Jacob soothed. "We'll get more things. Don't worry. They are just material things. This is temporary." In his heart, Jacob was devastated.

His father nodded and gave him a little smile and pat on the shoulder. Jacob felt weak in the knees like he might collapse, yet he was so full of adrenaline he could hardly hold still. Somebody had to be strong here. He would try to do that for the family.

He went to his room, taking a huge breath before entering. He knew what he would find, and he was not wrong. His room was a mess, and he couldn't even tell what all was missing. *What right do they have.....*

He stopped himself. He couldn't think like that. If he allowed himself to get angry he might do something foolish. He had seen what Nazis do to people who talk back to them. They don't stay alive five seconds following their outburst.

He sat down on his mattress, now missing its sheets. *God help us.* They were now out of Hitler's shadow and under his boot heel.

Following the occupation of Lodz, on September 14, 1939 was *Rosh Hashanah.*

Once again, Hitler demonstrated how low he would stoop. For this high holy day, he ordered businesses to stay open and the synagogues to be closed. He wouldn't even let them have their day of prayer.

The months following the attack had daily round-ups of Jews for forced labor. So far, the family had dodged those.

On November 7, Łódź was incorporated into the Third Reich and Hitler changed its name to *Litzmannstadt*.

On November 16, 1939 Hitler ordered Jews to wear an armband on their right arms. That was replaced by the yellow Star of David which became the rule on December 12.

All these losses hit Jacob and his siblings hard, but the memory of Mama's love and courage strengthened them.

They also would turn to God and each other to get through the dark times. And the times were about to get a lot darker.

CHAPTER 10

Good-Bye to a Way of Life   1939-1940

Jacob's pretty sister Fela and little dog
(Dr. Eisenbah's collection)

FORTUNATELY THE BOMBS DIDN'T DO massive damage in Jacob's city. There was concentrated bombing on their Air Force base. Some apartment buildings were hit; their roofs caved in and the walls crumbled in places, but the buildings proudly stood their ground. Factories were mostly left alone so the Nazis could plunder them.

The capitol, Warsaw, was occupied in 18 days. Much more damage was done there. Germans used their *Blitzkrieg* with frightening effectiveness. Extremely high-powered, they won quickly and with deadly might. They had motorcycles, tanks, machine guns, airplanes, everything.

When Nazi tanks rolled through, Polish Cavalry soldiers on horseback with their medieval lances could do nothing but gallop the opposite direction. The small army and few Polish tanks were a pathetic sight up against the might of the *Third Reich*.

Just as Jacob's friend Jack thought, Hitler had been quietly building war planes and artillery since shortly after he became Chancellor (their version of Vice President) in the early thirties. His adoring fans had no idea for a number of years what sort of a monster they had allowed to gain power. He didn't let them in on this until he was ready to strike. The Nazis knew exactly how to get the job done and in the wink of an eye Poland belonged to Hitler.

Fela was accepted at the Polish University of Poznan in Pharmacology and the family all shared her delight about it. But now she realized Hitler had something else in mind for her. So instead of college, she chose to flee to eastern Poland which the Russians were occupying. Though they were Hitler's allies, it was rumored they were easier on Jews than the Germans were.

"Don't go, Sweetheart," their father pleaded, his eyes so tired and sad. Repeatedly he asked her to stay.

"Papa, it will be all right. My friends Susanna and Marie are coming, too; I already have my train ticket. It will be an adventure." Her eyes were so bright and earnest.

"Don't worry so much; I'm old enough. You'll see, we'll be okay. A lot of Jews are leaving, Papa. You should think about going, too." She threw her arms around him in a big hug.

Such youthful optimism. Jacob wondered how close to being right she was. Should they all jump on a train? But Papa would never abandon his factory.

Papa barely acknowledged Fela's hug; he just stared out the window at the gray skies and people with tight faces hurrying by on their errands, trying to get off the streets as soon as possible. He had already lost his wife, now his only daughter.

Fela scampered off to pack a suitcase. Papa and the boys naturally worried they would never see her again, but she promised they would all meet up as soon as this was over. She would write them and that would help.

Papa somehow gathered his strength and resigned himself to it; they all walked her to the station when it was time. Things *had* to get better. They didn't know what to think; Hitler was like a reincarnated Attila the Hun.

In school Jacob learned in 441 Attila, one of the most feared and ruthless enemies of Rome, successfully invaded the eastern Roman Empire. Then he had the colossal nerve to attack Rome itself. That was his undoing; Rome's superior military skill was too much for him.

Perhaps Hitler had a bit of Attila in him; maybe he, too, would take on something too big and stumble. They could always hope.

They watched Fela board the train; their eyes followed as it pulled out of the station.

"Wave, Papa! There she is in the window." They tried to cheer him up, but he was just wrecked. He looked up and did a half-hearted wave and turned to leave. He walked slowly, a little more stooped. Still, there was nothing to do but move on.

He murmured "We need to have faith, boys. Hope for a better life will require belief in God's plan and the right actions." He walked at a turtle's speed and kept staring at the ground as he said these puzzling words.

What right actions? Jacob thought.

From that night forward, Papa seemed unable to move with any purpose; he would sit and stare at things. Jacob thought it was the evenings when Papa missed Mama and Fela the most. In the daytime he could go to work.

Meanwhile Jacob struggled fiercely with the new reality of daily life. His rational mind kept pounding away at him, trying to assume control. *It's going to get better. Murdering people in the streets can't be happening. This just doesn't happen in civilized countries.*

Jacob had seen too much to accept these thoughts without reservation. Things would get better, for sure; it was just a question of how many months or years it would take. How much mayhem would they have to witness before that beautiful day?

It wasn't long until Papa came in and collapsed in a chair one afternoon, tears running down his cheeks. Sam rushed over to him.

"What's wrong, Papa?" Sam's face was twisted in utter fright. He and Henry relied on their father to be strong. Jacob did too, but was capable of more independence. His heart broke for Papa and the boys.

"No one has money; there is no market for my linen products." He wiped some tears away. "So I had to shut down the factory. My employees and I were packing up things when Nazis swooped in like buzzards and picked it clean. They told us to get out of there so we did; I ran to the corner and watched them remove the machinery. They will send it all to Germany."

Sam just stared at him, mouth open.

Jacob rushed over to sit by his father. "Oh, Papa. It will be okay after we beat the tar out of Hitler. Everyone will start over. We'll all do it together and rebuild our country."

"I put everything I had into building that business. Now Nazis are going to get the rewards." Papa hung his head until his chin touched his chest. It didn't seem like he had the strength to lift it up again.

"I wasn't raised to expect anything like this. I was taught that if you worked hard and were good to your family, you would have a good life." Papa stared at his worn-out shoes. "Now I can't even buy a new pair of shoes."

He brooded a bit while the boys tried to think of something to say. "I'm so glad my parents and your mother didn't live to see this. Oh, my poor workers," he moaned. "They have no jobs now." Fresh tears came from his eyes.

Jacob thought about those workers. They loved Papa; he was kind and a good man to work for. Maybe they understood that he had no choice but to close the factory. He hoped they would be all right.

Papa's remark about the grandparents made Jacob sad. His beloved candy-store grandparents had died in the years before Hitler's assault on Poland; he missed them so much.

Papa wiped away some more tears with his sleeve.

Jacob looked at the floor; he couldn't watch Papa suffer. The Nazis were dismantling him a piece at a time, Jacob thought with rising fury. Papa's daughter fled; their town was besieged; their home was ransacked. The business was just another piece of him they took.

For a week Papa wandered around the house or sat and stared; he had no place to go to work anymore. Fortunately, life brightened up when a package arrived.

"Boys! Look! This came from Fela." Papa called out, his eyes alight. She included a letter; she was living in the large city of Lwów (Le-vov) in eastern Poland and liked it there.

They celebrated for a little while. There were biscuits, cheese, and some sausage. Sweet mustard and pickles; she even packed some cookies. It was a taste of home, of a way of life that was now gone.

Jacob wondered how she managed to get these things together in an occupied area. *The Russians must truly be kinder than the Germans,* he thought.

Their tormented family had no idea the next development would plunge them into another level of hell.

CHAPTER 11

The Ghetto: Heartbreak and Horror   1940-41

(5) German and Jewish police guard the Łódź ghetto entrance.

By December Jews were forced to wear the yellow Star of David. Boys in the street sold the badges. It was infuriating for Jacob to have to sew this mark of oppression on his own clothes. He wanted to throw up or scream out the window in outrage, but instead he helped the younger boys and Papa with their badges.

February 8, 1940: the German center of power brought the hammer down. Nazi soldiers were ordered to *Set up a Jewish ghetto in the oldest part of town and order all Jews to move in. Section it off with fencing. Install guard towers. Once it is sealed May 1, it will be death to any Jew not in the ghetto.*

The Nazis got busy. Jacob knew what they were doing; it was inconvenient to have to move, and a huge assault on their human rights, but it was worse than he knew. The ghetto would threaten their health, sanity and ultimately, their lives.

The day their family was ordered to go, they weren't given much time to pack. Jacob looked at the three boxes of his possessions. Was there anything else he couldn't live without? He scanned his room. No, he had his books, his clothes and shoes, his pictures, his favorite mementos. He had no bedding to pack except his pillow, and he would carry that under his arm.

Papa couldn't bring himself to go through Mama's things, so the boys did it for him. They packed her jewelry, pictures, books and mementos. They left her clothing and cosmetics there. They also scanned Fela's things to see if there was anything they should take. She had most of her clothes with her. They chose a few pictures, mementos and her graduation things.

Now they were ready. Even 12-year-old Henry was packed, though his boxes had things sticking out around the edges and were piled too high to fold the tops down. He had toy boats in his pockets and was carrying several stuffed toys and his pillow. They would put what blankets they had left over the bundle in the cart.

We'll put his lop-sided boxes on top of the other stuff, Jacob thought, and chuckled. *That crazy kid.*

They had twelve boxes, two packed suitcases and a few pieces of furniture: two beds, a couch, a table and chairs, a chest of drawers, lamps, a few kitchen things plus a little food. They would have to leave everything else; they were assigned to a cramped one-room apartment.

It didn't matter what they left. The beautiful pieces of furniture were taken by the Nazis already, along with their silver, wedding china and anything exquisite; even their paintings. It was a devastating blow that brought Papa down, hard. He had so prided himself in what he provided for his family.

They began pulling their possessions to the ghetto in their cart. It took a number of exhausting trips down the streets over to their new home, their prison. There was barely room to turn around in the one-room apartment. Once they put everything away the following day, it was a little better but they were tightly crowded.

Outside, every 200 feet were watch towers stocked with guards, weapons and hate. Walking around, Jacob and his brothers stared up at a tower and its searchlights. A guard was stationed there with a machine gun. They took a few steps backward; it was scary being that close to his gun.

"How will we find our aunts and uncles?" Sam asked Papa.

"We traded addresses before we left. Those who don't have their new addresses yet will contact one of us and we'll help them locate the others."

They had no phones, bicycles, buses, newspapers, or radios; restrictions were tightening around them like a noose. Before long, incoming mail would be stopped.

In April a fence went up surrounding the ghetto. On May 1, the ghetto was 'sealed'. From that day on, they were prisoners in their own city and the food supply began to dwindle.

There were some empty pieces of land inside. The Jewish ghetto administration announced that anyone who worked the land could have a piece of it. The family went in together with other family members and friends to sign up for land. They set to work planting food. The Jewish administration provided the seeds for a few coins.

There were already some fruit trees there: apples, pears and cherries. They planted potatoes, tomatoes, carrots, and beets. This extra food would help them survive and they were determined to use it very sparingly. It lasted for months when harvested.

One evening the family was eating supper. Papa was morose, as usual. Jacob tried to cheer him. "Papa, I still plan to go to dental school. Are you excited for me? I am only two years away from it."

"Yes, Kuba. You will love being a dentist," he said woodenly.

"I hate those guards," said Henry, as he stabbed his vegetables with a fork. I want to throw a big rock at them in their stupid towers."

"Don't do that, please," Jacob warned. "They will shoot you. Please don't do anything to make them look at you. We have to be invisible."

"Like the *Invisible Man*? How?"

"No, Henry," sighed Sam. "He means keep your head down and don't make trouble."

"I don't make trouble," said Henry, looking wounded.

Papa said "Son, you must keep safe. You stay here with me. I'll make sure you don't become a target."

"A target?" Henry's eyes were huge now.

"I meant to say, I'll make sure no one wants to hurt you, okay?"

Henry nodded, but stared at his vegetables. Jacob wanted to shoot every last Nazi out there. How *dare they* frighten his brother like this? He was only a kid.

"After we eat let's build a bridge with your building set, okay?" Jacob said.

"Super," Henry grinned. He had been sheltered and taken care of very well. As the baby of the family, he took his time growing up. He hadn't discovered girls yet, something that couldn't be said about Jacob at that age.

I wonder if he'll be an engineer or builder someday. He likes to put things together, Jacob thought.

They received food-ration cards. The cards had the word 'Jew' stamped on them. He felt like a piece of meat with its grade stamped on it. He didn't know that Jews received half as much food as non-Jews outside the ghetto. What he did know was that people were starving. The big men began to die first, because they got no more food than anyone else. They would just fall down in the street and die.

In spite of all their fears, one evening Sam said "I feel safer now, don't you Papa?"

"In what way, Son?"

"Those Jew-killers can't come in the ghetto. That's what the guys at school say."

"You're right; we don't have to go out in groups anymore. I guess that's one piece of luck," Papa said.

"I wouldn't say *totally relax,*" said Jacob, using his father's line, "because they might sneak in here."

"Why would they risk it?" asked Papa. "If they were mistaken for Jews, they would be shot on sight leaving the ghetto." The children agreed.

The Jews didn't know they were *not* safe. They were in a holding place, warehoused until the Nazis could decide how to get rid of them, all 180,000 to 200,000 of them. The numbers varied month to month. Their city had many factories and Jews from other areas were shipped in to work, and of course many were shipped out to die.

When going on an errand or to school, Jacob sometimes had to step around a body. It was always jarring when he realized he was looking at a dead person, even though it was a common sight.

These victims would crumple half-way in the street and half on the sidewalk, or leaning up against a wall. When they fell in doorways it was heartbreaking to have to step over them to go inside. The bodies lay there until groups of Jews came and took them reverently up the hill to the Łódź cemetery.

He hadn't yet located his best friend Jack. He had tried to call him before they moved but they didn't answer. He would not see Jack Sieradski until after the war. Somehow he escaped the nightmare of the ghetto, perhaps by going into hiding somewhere; Jacob doesn't remember the specifics, but Jack survived the war.

Meanwhile, he made a new friend named David. He was two years older than Jacob and had graduated from high school. He was a very entertaining guy. They visited each other frequently and became close friends.

"How does Hitler make those young girls swoon?" David asked one night at Jacob's apartment. "We're way better looking than he is."

Jacob laughed. "I'm sorry to see your confidence at such a low point."

"All right, I know it sounds cocky. But what the heck? The man is in his forties and young girls are swooning over him, like he's some matinee idol. I saw it on those newsreels. When we still had newspapers I read an article about him that said he urges young girls to get pregnant and calls unwed mothers his *brides*. We should be so lucky to have a hundred brides who worship us and not even have to support them."

"Your mind goes some strange places," laughed Jacob. "Personally, the *last thing* I want is a hundred wives." He shook his head; *that guy is crazy*.

"Did I tell you about my mother's friend who went to the Summer Olympics in 1936 in Berlin?

"No."

"Well, first of all, she isn't Jewish so there was no problem about her crossing the border. She was shocked to see all that Hitler-worship on the streets; everywhere she looked."

"I can imagine. Nauseating." Jacob shook his head. "What do you make of that ugly little Goebbels? He is one of the top guys and does all that propaganda stuff yet he has the stupidest personality, doesn't he?"

"Yes," said David. "The word '*starch*' comes to mind." He began marching smartly back and forth; Papa and the boys were there and looked on in amusement. David stopped and did a smart *Heil Hitler* salute. "Hello, I'm Joseph Goebbels and I have a club foot. I am here to promote the Nazi party's policy on *ostracizing handicapped people.*"

They howled in laughter. It was beyond ridiculous.

"Look below your knees, Goebbels!" Jacob called out.

"Hitler hasn't noticed this little problem with *mein* foot," responded David, with a thick accent.

Even Papa laughed.

A few weeks later, just about the time Jacob was starting to get used to life in the ghetto, Papa walked in the door with a horrified look on his face.

"What's wrong, Papa?" his youngest son ran to him.

"Nothing, Son, run along outside and play. I just have a headache." He signaled with his eyes for Jacob to join him over in the kitchen area, while Henry went outside.

"Where did Sam go?"

"Outside with friends," said Jacob, scanning his father's tense face. *What happened?* He was almost afraid to ask.

Papa broke down into heaving sobs. Jacob reached out and put his hand on Papa's shoulder.

"I told him. That crazy, stubborn Zajdel. I told him to get rid of that radio, but he brought it along with him into the ghetto. Someone turned him in."

"No! Who would do that?" Jacob gasped, hoping desperately they could get Uncle Zajdel out of jail before the Nazis hurt him. "How can we help him?"

"Help?" Papa looked at him, hurt radiating from his eyes. "They came in his house and shot him in front of his wife. There's no helping him."

Jacob gasped; he couldn't speak. Hot tears were coming, and he tried to hold back.

"My little brother always had to do things his own way. He was so stubborn," Papa moaned. "I can't believe life has come to this. To be executed for having a radio. Our world has gone mad, and the rest of the world is equally insane for allowing this to happen." His face was already pale and hollow from hunger; now there was a new layer of anxiety.

"Papa," Jacob hurried to fix it. "Maybe we can help his wife. Oh, poor Aunt Anne. What should we do?" Activity was always helpful.

"Do you want to come with me?" Papa asked. "I'm going over to see her. She's being taken care of by friends and neighbors. We can't do much for her. Thank God they didn't shoot her, too."

Jacob shuddered. The casual use of those words clearly showed how insane their world had become. "Yes, I'll go with you. Are you going to tell Sam and Henry?"

"I don't think they're ready to hear it yet. Especially Henry, but I don't want to leave them here by themselves. If they come with us obviously they'll know what happened."

"They are tougher than they look, Papa. Let me fix you something to eat. Would you like a glass of juice?" They had no wine in the ghetto. No alcoholic beverages, not even coffee or tea. People made a type of coffee out of beets that tasted terrible.

Papa accepted the offer gratefully and Jacob poured him a glass of apple juice diluted with water. "I don't know if it's a good or a bad thing he didn't have children," Papa said, as he took the glass and began to sip the juice.

"I don't know, either," Jacob said, but he thought probably it was a good thing, because look how Papa now had to struggle to provide for three boys. They were all starving and Papa couldn't do anything about it. Of course he would never tell his father that.

Jacob thought about Uncle Zajdel. He used to work in a factory, making sweaters. He liked to know what was going on in the world, and the radio was a lifeline. Unfortunately, having one carried a death sentence.

Life was far more terrifying than the most dramatic horror films he'd seen. This was *real*.

He would miss him so much. He was their favorite uncle because of his warmth and funny jokes; a very caring man and a great conversationalist. There was a huge hole in the family, where Zajdel had lived and spread his sunshine.

The family ate some small sandwiches and then walked over to Zajdel's apartment, ten minutes away. Papa brought along some pears to give Aunt Anne. He explained to the younger boys as gently as he could that Uncle Zajdel went to be with God today.

Henry screamed "NO!! Why, Papa?"

"Because it is God's will. I'm sorry to have to tell you this terrible thing, but he was shot by the Nazis because he had a radio."

They stared at him, unblinking. "A radio?" Henry said. "What's so bad about that?"

"It's illegal," said Sam, brushing tears away on his sleeve.

"You have to follow rules around here. They don't give second chances," said Papa, putting his arm around Henry. "I'm so sad, too. He was my little brother. We're going over to try to help Aunt Anne."

The younger boys started to walk again. They kept their eyes down, their fright and confusion plain to see.

All of them were becoming so shell-shocked, hearing about or seeing atrocities daily wasn't much of a surprise anymore. But when it struck this close to home....

Jacob worried about his brothers' mental health. As for himself, he was strong; he'd be all right, but they were more vulnerable.

Aunt Anne was sitting on a couch with neighbors and friends, crying hysterically. Papa walked over to her and held out his arms. She stood up and hugged him.

"We are in such danger; we never know if we will be alive tomorrow. We have to rely on God," Papa said. "I'm so sorry, Annie. He was my little brother and I loved him very much."

The boys watched Papa comforting their aunt and remained quiet. Finally she offered them some precious treats that were brought to her by friends and family for this sorrowful occasion.

The boys were grateful; food was always soothing. They went to the table and looked over the items. They took a little fruit and some sweetened cheese and sat on the couch to eat it, not knowing what to say or do for their aunt. Jacob hoped just being there would help.

Inch by inch, the horrors crept up on them. Each time they somehow adjusted to it, and each time they soon experienced more.

They tried to have *Shabbot* every week, but there was little food, and it was just too hard to manage. Half of the spirit of it was gone without Mama and Fela.

Jacob had met another friend in the ghetto, Ben. One day he asked Jacob "Why don't we just cut a hole in the fence and escape? We could go to Switzerland or somewhere."

"That's suicide," commented Jacob. "You're not stupid enough to try that, are you?"

"No. I just like to talk big."

Jacob chuckled. "I hope so. I could never attempt an escape. Look at this." Jacob lifted a pant leg and pointed to his swollen lower leg. "This is from starvation. I wouldn't be able to fight even if I wasn't afraid of their guns."

"Oh, that's bad, Kuba. What are you doing for it?"

"Nothing, Ben. I try not to look at my legs. I'm hoping it just gets better. I don't want to go in the hospital. I wouldn't feel safe there." He glanced at his friend's legs. "Don't you have swelling?"

"No, so far I just have stomach cramps and headaches. What if your swelling gets worse?"

"If it goes up to my heart, I'll die, so I guess I'll have to go to the hospital before that, but not yet." Jacob wanted to get off the subject. "Let's go toss a ball around," he said.

They had two hospitals in the ghetto with their own doctors and dentists. But there was a tough downside: they had no anesthesia.

When they first moved into the ghetto, Fela continued to write from eastern Poland, and sent food. Her little notes and packages were greeted by joyful shouts; Papa would perk up for a bit.

After a few months the packages stopped abruptly. More and more life drained from Papa as the days went by. They considered the awful implication.

Fela might not be alive.

In May when they sealed the ghetto, incoming mail was banned, so they had no further hope of hearing from her. Sam and Jacob let Papa and Henry think she might have met a man and moved somewhere. The older boys were more realistic, but of course, they didn't know for sure. They kept her close in their hearts and hoped for the best.

They tried to map out a plan for the future, but everything was so wildly unstable. Slowly, they let go of their dreams and began to live one day at a time, if one could call that *living.*

One day David and Jacob talked about finding work. Jacob was 17, David 19. They considered the factories in the ghetto that manufactured war materials. David decided to work in one of them. Maybe he wouldn't go on the Nazi train if he was working there.

Each factory had a kitchen, which served watery soup, like the hospitals and prison camps. The kitchens had a central office where Jacob wanted to work. He could get some extra money and maybe somehow get some extra food, even if only from the trash.

After their short visit, Jacob left David's apartment and went home to check on Henry, who was weak and tired a lot from starvation. Even with that little bit of extra food from their garden, he was not thriving.

His brothers meant the world to Jacob, and he wouldn't even consider the thought that Henry might not survive. Tragically, the chain of events that led to Henry's great peril had already begun.

CHAPTER 12

Like Herring In A Barrell   1942-1943

Jacob's youngest brother Henry
(Dr. Eisenbach's collection)

A tattered photo of Sam
(Dr. Eisenbach's collection)

THE DOCTOR WAS AT THE apartment when Jacob returned.

"What do you think, Doctor?" asked Papa.

Jacob's head spun. *Please, no more bad news.*

The doctor looked pained to say it. "I'm not sure. Henry might have Tuberculosis."

Papa put his head down and shook it. Jacob jumped in. "What do we do, Doctor?"

"I recommend sending him daily to this treatment center." He hand-ed them a card. "They'll give him a little extra food, and there will be other young people there for him to be with."

Henry looked so frail, his eyes seeming too large for his thin face.

Jacob was a young man of action. He had to bring in some money and somehow get more food for Henry, if possible. And Papa – God help him. Jacob didn't have the luxury of worrying and grieving.

So he focused on getting that job in the ghetto kitchen. Chief Rumkowski, the Jewish head of the ghetto, visited the outpatient center regularly. Jacob wrote him a letter asking for the job, and sent it with Henry. Action always helped keep him together emotionally, even the smallest accomplishments.

"How long does Henry have to go to that outpatient place?" He asked Papa one day.

"Until he is stronger."

"I worry about him. He's so young," Jacob said with rare candor around Papa.

Sitting on the couch, Papa turned his gaze toward Jacob with a help-less expression, but said nothing.

Jacob wished he had kept his feelings to himself. Papa couldn't han-dle all this. From that point on, he was determined to put on a brave face for Papa and the boys.

Two weeks later the kitchen supervisor called and gave Jacob the job. He rejoiced: one small victory, but the pay was *peanuts*. Too bad it wasn't literally peanuts; they could have eaten those.

He loved staying busy. He moved around the office with zeal and made sure kitchens got supplies and utensils. Sometimes shortages prevented him from filling the orders, but he always tried. Even though he worked for the kitchens, he didn't steal food. That carried an immediate death sentence. There was precious little food thrown in the trash that he could scavenge.

They still had school, which he enjoyed. He finished high school in the ghetto. They had some of the same teachers, and it was still a strong education.

And *girls;* that usually went smoothly.

"So, Kuba, any new women in your life lately?" David enjoyed teasing him about his romantic endeavors.

"I met a few girls and spent time with a couple of them," he said. Gentlemen didn't share details, so he hoped David wouldn't ask.

But red-blooded David *did* ask. "Tell me. What were they like? What happened?"

"You need to find your own girls. I don't spill the beans and I don't do anything you don't."

"How do you know what I do?"

"Wild guess. I know you, David," he chuckled.

In 1942 Jacob met a striking girl named Claire. He was almost 19 and she was 18. She would become important to him.

They had been in the ghetto two years, but he'd never seen her before. She was lovely and like he most desired, highly intelligent. She had long, shiny hair, the darkest shade of mahogany. Her playful brown eyes sparkled with wit. She was great company, and a good sport if she lost at cards or word games. She was upbeat, like him. His only complaint: she was shy about returning affection. He would have to remedy that.

Jacob and Claire would get together with friends and have intellectual discussions or play cards. Being young, they found ways to ignore the obvious crisis and enjoy themselves. Romance could blossom in the most depressing surroundings, and it did, to Jacob's delight.

He invited her to visit; the family was impressed by her good manners and polite conversation. She held her drink daintily, a mixture of juice and water. She laughed at Papa's old thread-bare jokes. Her visits seemed to cheer him; maybe he was imagining new footsteps toddling around him and playful tugs at his hair from chubby little hands.

One day they walked to a park to sit and chat. She opened the gate; Jacob stepped behind her and took it. "Ladies first," he said like a knight in King Arthur's court.

She smiled back and went in. They settled on the grass. He held her hand, so dainty and white. Her hair was beautiful; he took a lock of it and felt the softness. "You do a great job with this. My sister likes to do hair, too."

Her face colored a bit. "I am thinking of being a beautician, so I practice."

"If you make them as pretty as you, they'll love you."

She blushed again and changed the subject. "What shall we talk about?"

They explored their favorite movies and music. It turned out they shared many interests. Jacob loved the sound of violins and always wanted to learn to play, though he never did. Like him, she loved Viennese music and modern American swing, though she no longer had a radio.

Maybe because of his compliments, she gave him a sweet good-bye kiss that day. Dare he hope for a future with her? He tried not to think about it. Right now he had far too much to deal with just to survive.

———— ⤜∽⤛ ————

One day Heinrich Himmler, number 2 man in the Reich, came to inspect the ghetto. Totally impressed with his own awesomeness, Himmler walked crisply down the street in his black SS uniform, looking over the soldiers and making sure Jews weren't getting away with anything.

If one soldier had a wrinkled shirt or his shoes weren't sparkling, he'd scream at him or have his thugs beat him with batons. Jacob burned with rage. How did God allow this demon to strut around like that, unharmed? His arrogance was staggering; an evil peacock showing off his feathers.

No, fumed Jacob. *Not a peacock; no animal is that evil. Even snakes don't go around hurting their victims just to have a good time or impress other snakes.*

Himmler had a world-class ego. He would do *anything* to secure his power and prestige. He was responsible for much of the slaughter of the Jews. He oversaw the SS killing squads and the concentration camps. Jacob heard far too many horror stories whispered about Heinrich Himmler.

Without him, Jacob wondered if Hitler would even be effective. He needed a smart right-hand man who had no conscience of any kind, and in Himmler, that's exactly what he got.

Adolf Hitler had no children though he loved them and would sometimes hold one of his inner circle's children on his lap during meetings.

Heinrich Himmler had a daughter he adored. Jacob could never figure out how these family-loving guys could kill women and children. He thought probably because to Nazis, Jews were not really *human beings*. They were just dirty vermin, disposable lumps of flesh.

The SS, the elite volunteer army of killers dressed in black with a *death's head* (skull and crossbones) on their uniforms and hats, were styled to intimidate, all at least six feet tall. They even had a bold flag, all black with shining skull and bones.

"That stupid SS thing looks like a pirate flag," Henry said one day while lining up his three little model ships on the chest of drawers.

"Perfect," said Jacob. "They plunder and murder just like them."

In 1942 there was a deadly typhus epidemic. 15-year-old Henry developed a high fever; the doctor said to get him to the hospital immediately.

Papa didn't go with them; he was neither mentally nor physically strong enough. Jacob worried Papa wouldn't last much longer; he was so burdened with sorrow. At least the boys had the resilience of youth.

"Don't worry, Papa. Sam and I will take him and get him all settled in. Henry will be fine. I'll visit him every day."

Papa nodded absently.

So Sam and Jacob went with Henry, supporting him as he stumbled along, falling every few steps. He complained a little from hunger and sickness. While he soothed Henry, Jacob mentally cursed Hitler and imagined him in sixty different kinds of hell.

When they arrived, they got Henry set up in a clean room. He looked so pale and small against those white sheets. Jacob poured him a glass of cool water and set it by his bedside.

"Just think about getting better, Henry. I'll be back tomorrow to visit." he said. "I'll bring you some fruit."

"Try to rest and read; here are some books for you." Sam held out some of his favorites.

Henry sat up and pleaded. "Don't leave me. What will happen? Will they hurt me?"

Shaken, Jacob was quick to respond. "No, you'll be okay. I'll come every day. We love you; I'll look out for you. Papa is not feeling well, but he will come sometimes, too. While you're resting you can read these. See?" He pointed to where Sam had put the books on the table next to the bed.

Henry looked at them, nodded and slumped back.

It was all Jacob could do to turn and leave him there, but he had to. The hospital was a contagious place. He couldn't afford to get sick. Who would take care of the family? And he didn't want to lose his job.

Several days later, it was September 1, 1942; three years from the day Hitler invaded. In those three years, their only loss to Hitler was Fela, if she wasn't alive, and Zajdel.

Please, let there be no more, was Jacob's constant prayer.

As he walked to work he passed the hospital where Henry was housed. German trucks were standing in front, guarded by Nazis with their frightening guns. A few years earlier their behavior would have utterly shocked him. Now, it wasn't that much of a surprise. While one truck pulled out, soldiers carried out sick people from the hospital and *stacked them up* in the back of the other truck.

Jacob didn't know what was happening, but knew it was terrible. He ran like a frightened cheetah toward the one pulling out.

Two German soldiers were in the cab of the truck, one driving while the other held a gun. The Nazis lent their own special flavor to the term 'riding shotgun', tattooing innocents with bullet holes.

Sick patients were in the back of the truck, in stacks of *twenty*. *Like herring in a barrel,* Jacob thought with mounting fury. They were *alive and moving around.*

How does the person on the bottom not get crushed to death? He wondered, frantically trying to peer into the truck bed as he ran alongside.

Was Henry there? There was no time to get a good look. The soldier took aim at him and began shooting; Jacob raced into an apartment building and they drove away.

He leaned against the wall, taking huge gulps of air. He had literally dodged a bullet; how much more terror would they have to endure? His hands shook; he ran his fingers through his hair. Poor little Henry wouldn't dodge *this* bullet unless he could get him out of there.

Jacob went around to the back of the hospital. Nurses were handing patients over a tall fence to a crowd of Jews.

He didn't have long legs, but he scaled that 9-foot fence like a cat up a tree. He flew into the hospital and down to the kitchen where he grabbed a chef's smock and put it on as a disguise. It was like some old spy movie, but it was horribly real.

There were no elevators, so wearing his chef's costume he climbed the stairs; a doctor passed him. He looked at Jacob like 'Who are YOU?' but said nothing. In Nazi territory the less said, the better.

He raced into the room where he had visited Henry the night before. He leaned against the door, gasping with oxygen-starved lungs, staring in despair at the empty beds. He asked about Henry and the nurse looked at him with big, sad eyes.

"He was carried out 15 minutes ago."

Jacob's heart broke and lay in his chest in pieces. *15 minutes?* It might as well have been a year.

He felt trapped in tentacles of horror: his little brother was in one of those trucks. Jacob wondered if Henry saw him when he was trying to find him. He hoped so. Now he wouldn't be able to get him out of there, even if he was still out front in the second truck. They would kill him if he tried.

"Where are they taking them?"

"I'm sorry, I wish I could tell you. We don't really know, so we're just trying to get the patients out of here."

"Yes, I saw that out back. Do you think they will take them to the camps?" he asked, trying to ignore the dull roar in his head.

"I don't know; I'm so sorry." She looked kindly at him, though she was distraught, too. He needed a hug; but instead he just thanked her and hurried out the door.

As he exited the hospital, he saw that both trucks were gone.

The thought tried to come up. *You said you'd look after him. You let him down.*

He pushed it aside. *No, I didn't. I almost took a bullet trying to save him. No one can stop the Nazis. It's not my fault, it's theirs. They are vicious, murdering monsters.*

White-hot pain seared his heart. What would happen to Henry? He ran through the scenarios. *They might make him work for them in the camp. Maybe because he's so young, they will spare him.* His rational mind suspected otherwise, but it was staying out of this.

He started the walk home, wondering how he was going to tell Papa. He needed some tender care himself. He thought of Claire; he would go over there first. Hearing what he went through, hopefully she would hug him and give him the nurturing he needed so much right now.

The thought of seeing Claire made his heart skip a beat. He briefly wondered about romantic love. Is this what it felt like? If this was love, it was pretty darned good.

He didn't feel good for long, though. As he walked, thoughts of Henry tortured him, choking him with outrage. He was only four when Henry was born but he remembered what a sweet little bundle he was. His frequent smiles and gentle cooing added even more happiness to their home.

He recalled the day they went ice skating and Henry knocked down the other skater. Henry sloshing along in the rain puddles. Packing his things all crazy in those boxes. Being angry at the guards in the tower.

Trusting his father and falling asleep the night of the bombing. Crying for his mother.

Jacob began to sob, huge keening cries coming from deep in his soul. He allowed himself the luxury at first but soon stopped, remembering he was now the family's strength.

Poor Papa was just reeling with all these losses; his home, his factory, his wife, his daughter, his brother Zajdel and now his son. Jacob worried it would kill Papa, but somehow he had to go home, break the news, and find a way to comfort him.

Right after he saw Claire.

CHAPTER 13

Please, Not Papa   1942-1943

*(6) Ghetto Litzmannstadt (Łódź): Children being sent to the
Chelmno Death camp. The guard appears so relaxed. Just
another boring day at work. Many thousands of these
children were gassed; the poor little innocents
appear to be about 5 years old.*

HE FELT A LITTLE BETTER when he neared Claire's apartment; he turned
the corner and hurried to her building. He ran up the stairs and down
the hall, his heart pounding wildly in love's sweet anticipation.

When he got there, it was locked up.

"*NO!!*" He screamed. He pounded on the door anyway, calling her name. No one answered. What did that mean?

Not Claire! His insides cried out.

He ran to the neighbor's apartment and banged on the door. The old woman took her time shuffling to the door. She opened it a couple of inches and peered at him.

"Where is Claire?" He almost shouted. "I saw her only a few days ago."

"They're gone. I am sorry."

"Are you sure?" He asked, his eyes begging her to change the story.

"I'm sorry. The whole family left together."

No! Not the Nazi train.

"Do you think they ran away or did they go on the train?"

"I believe they were being deported. That is what the gentleman told the grocer."

So the Nazi train, then. Jacob thanked her and turned away. He stared at Claire's apartment with its padlock. *Those murdering beasts.*

Oh, Claire. Where are you and what are you going through? He sent her his loving thoughts and asked God to please keep her safe.

Outside he collapsed on the front steps and sat with his head in his hands. This must be hell. He and all the other Jews must be dead and now in hell, though he didn't understand *why*. Weren't you supposed to *deserve* it if you went there? Jews had done nothing to bring on this catastrophe that shredded their lives.

After a while, he got up and walked slowly home. Sometimes he almost didn't care what happened to him anymore, but he wouldn't allow himself to fold up. He began to pray and got some strength. Sam and Papa would need support. Mama wouldn't want him to give up, either. She had said the Nazis couldn't have her children or her husband and he was going to do his best to make sure they didn't get any more of them.

He braced himself and went into the apartment. Papa was sitting at the table, picking at some lunch and glanced over at Jacob blankly. He didn't expect him back from work this soon, so he probably dreaded what Jacob had to say. He looked to be in a kind of stupor, keeping a protective shell around himself.

Jacob tried to break through it. "Papa, I have some news of Henry. He was taken by the Nazis today out of the hospital to a different location for treatment." Papa just stared, not twitching a muscle. He wasn't fooled by Jacob's attempt to soften the blow.

"My son is gone." He said simply and pushed his plate away.

Jacob ran to Papa and embraced him. They both cried. Sam got home from school and wanted to know what happened. When he heard, he curled his hands into fists and looked like he could kill someone. Jacob put his arm around him, too, and the three of them held each other and cried.

He couldn't bring himself to tell them about Claire yet. They liked her so much, particularly Papa. It was too much for them on top of the news about Henry.

Thanks to the railroad guys sharing what they knew, Jews surmised mass murder was going on. The method was apparently poisonous gas, then they burned the bodies. He'd heard about the terrible smoke stacks with their tell-tale smell of burning flesh.

So Henry was probably gassed. Why else would they remove patients from the hospital? They weren't well enough to work for the Nazis somewhere. This would be the end of Henry. His rational mind prevailed, and it devastated him.

Grief spread its dark wings over the family during the following weeks. There would be no funeral for Henry; no gravestone to visit. He was just a puff of smoke now, perhaps on his way to heaven, or maybe he went there instantly. There wasn't much else they could do but struggle for survival and grieve their losses.

Every time he looked at Henry's little ships he almost broke down. However, in spite of what his rational mind said, there was a slight chance Henry was alive in a camp somewhere. He *had* to be. No one should have to suffer this much loss, over and over. Surely God would step in somewhere. That's what his intuitive, creative and spiritual mind told him, and he preferred to listen to that part of himself at the moment.

One evening while he was preparing some boiled potatoes, cheese and tomatoes, Jacob suddenly felt overwhelmed again. *Can we possibly heal from this nightmare? Is it worth it to go on living?* He walked away from the stove and looked out the window.

Yes, it was. Mama had taught them they were worth more than that. She was watching over them and he would not let her down. Jacob's will to survive and belief in an eventual positive outcome soon returned to brighten his days a little.

—∞∞∞—

Children were rounded up from the Litzmannstasdt (Łódź) Ghetto, in the thousands for transport, along with the elderly. Jacob was spared the pain of seeing this line of condemned Jewish children in his ghetto. He only found out after the war about the full extent of the atrocities.

Mercifully, he didn't know Hitler had built a concentration camp *for children of non-Jewish Poles* who had been murdered in clearing the land for German occupation. He also didn't know the killing of large groups of children was sometimes handled by firing squads or they would throw grenades into a group of them.

The killing squads continued right through the end of the war, even though gas became the preferred method for dispatching large numbers of people. They sometimes pushed the job of shooting children onto someone else like Ukranians, because the work became too disgusting, even for the Nazis. Once when Heinrich Himmler watched a siege of executions of adults and their children by rifle squad, he ran around screaming 'Kill them quickly'. He couldn't stand to watch it. Himmler having a soft spot? That was rare, to say the least.

Jacob didn't know about all of that, but he did know about the Warsaw Uprising. April 19 – May 16 of 1943 the brave people in the

Warsaw ghetto stood up to the Nazis. Word spread about it and somehow got past the Nazis into the ghetto. Jacob was so proud of them. The Warsaw Jews knew all of this was a death sentence, so why not go down fighting?

They had a few weapons and managed to fight back for *thirty days* before the inevitable Nazi victory. It was a stellar effort. Though the Nazis brought airplanes and all their might against them, the people didn't cave in immediately. They were incredibly heroic.

Surprisingly, the Nazis lost a *huge number* of soldiers in that battle. Not all the rebels died, and the survivors were marched off to die in a camp. At least they made their stand. Uncle Zajdel, Henry, Claire and maybe Fela got to make no such stand.

⸎

Then the inevitable black day arrived in 1943; it was like a morgue in the apartment. The summons had come for Papa; he just gave in. The boys had never seen him without one drop of fight in him; Hitler had broken him. Sam and Jacob, their poor hearts and minds scattered over forty acres, clung to him that evening and promised they'd hold out until everyone could reunite.

"We'll be all right, Papa. We'll survive," Jacob said. Papa didn't respond. He just weakly put his arms around the boys' shoulders and stood there, tears rolling down his cheeks. Once again, Jacob wanted to kill every Nazi he could find.

Later Jacob was in bed, gathering courage for the morning.

PLEASE, NOT PAPA! He begged God to spare him. Then he had a talk with himself.

We'll survive this, I know; somehow, some way, we will live through it. Papa will be all right; he's always been a strong man. The war will have to end sometime. Tomorrow we'll give him all our love to take with him.

He turned out the light and closed his eyes, eager to escape this living nightmare for a few hours.

Next morning Papa embraced them, more haggard and aged than ever. He looked like he'd been up all night. Again Jacob tried to be strong for him. Papa looked at them like he was studying their features. He knew Papa was thinking '*Is today the last time I'll look upon my sons' faces?*'

"It will be okay, Papa." Sam said in a small voice.

"It will," Jacob chimed in. "I'll take care of Sam and we'll be here waiting for everyone to return after we defeat Hitler. You just take care of yourself and rest as much as you can." He put on his most serious face so Papa could see he was capable of taking over for him.

Papa nodded at him and murmured "It's time to go." He picked up his suitcase and weaved a bit, unsteady on his feet.

Jacob gently took it from him. "I'll get this," he said, hoping Papa could feel his love. "Come on, now. We'll go with you."

At the station, they said their tear-soaked good-byes. The Nazis took Papa's luggage from him and ordered him to go to the boxcar area. Jacob and Sam trembled at the nearness of these evil creatures, so close the boys caught a whiff of their sickly sweet after-shave. They hurried away to watch from a safe distance. They saw Papa climb up into the boxcar and disappear into the crowd of people inside. Sam began to sob; Jacob rubbed his back.

The train squealed, then huffed and chuffed; finally it pulled away from the station slowly, as if it didn't want to make this trip; like it was being forced to participate in Hitler's evil deeds, the same as everyone else. The train finally picked up some speed and Papa's car was no longer in sight. All the luggage was left standing at the station.

"Look, Kuba. The luggage; they forgot it."

"I doubt they *forgot* it. They're probably just going to keep it and steal their stuff."

They turned around, orphaned by the hurricane that was Nazi Germany. They walked home in a daze, trying to keep their shattered minds focused on watching for roaming anti-Semites with murderous intent. Maybe somehow they got inside the ghetto; Jews could never feel secure.

The boys had to get their own food at the store now. They hadn't been taught to cook, so they struggled with it. Jacob found some potato peelings in a bucket on the back step of a restaurant. That night he boiled them and tried to eat them; they were so hungry all the time. It wasn't long before he was throwing up. They were the bitterest things he ever tried to eat. Thankfully Sam hadn't eaten any.

Eating had lost its pleasure, anyway. They ate the cereal and the bread, the raisins and the corn, and similar staples; no gourmet pastry treats for them. And no more of Mama's delicious *cholent*. Ever again.

One day Sam was staring at his meager lunch.

"It will turn out all right, Sam." Jacob said. "After Hitler loses the war we'll find Papa, Fela and Henry, too. They are stronger than Hitler; they'll stay alive. He doesn't believe in God, so just from *that* we know we're stronger than Hitler."

Sam took a listless bite.

"So please eat and keep your strength up. They're going to need us to help them get better. And imagine! You might be an uncle; maybe Fela got married and has some nephews for us!"

"Or nieces," Sam said, continuing to munch carrots.

Jacob got up to get some milk for them. "Yes, nieces too; we'll love them so much. We'll teach the boys to play ball, and we will read stories to the little girls." He poured milk into Sam's glass. "Don't go anywhere after school today, Sam. Come straight home. I don't think it's a good idea anymore to be alone on the streets unless it's absolutely necessary. The neighbors are home if you need anything. You'll be okay while I go to work?"

Sam nodded and continued to chew his food glumly. His big brother, now officially man of the house, looked away and prayed.

Jacob and cousin Schmul saw each other every day; at one or the other's apartments or around town. Now Jacob realized he hadn't seen Schmul in a week. He had a bad feeling about it, but thought there was some reasonable explanation. Maybe he was sick. *Please don't let it be Typhus*, he prayed.

After another two days, they decided to go check on him. When he and Sam got there, they found Schmul's apartment locked up.

Oh, God, not Schmul, too. They ran to the neighbor's but they weren't home, either. They weren't able to find anyone to ask. Nazis must have cleared out the whole apartment building.

Jacob sat down on the curb and put his head in his hands. Again he thought *This must be hell. Have all the Jews died and we are in some ungodly hell?*

He just could not take another death.

Sam talked with him a while, trying to encourage him, which was a valiant effort; Sam was more often hand-wringing and grief-stricken, sensitive and so hurt.

It was too cold to stay out very long. They began the walk home. If Jacob had learned anything from all this, it was that one has to accept the unacceptable sometimes. And go on.

CHAPTER 14

Teenage Fugitives   March/1944

*(7) Rumkowski, Jewish Chief of the Łódź ghetto, who gave Jacob a job.
He was betrayed by the Nazis after fulfilling their evil orders.*

LIFE WENT ON AND THE two boys somehow adjusted to the *new normal* until March, 1944. Then like a violent earthquake, their world was shaken upside-down again. Jacob was now fighting for his life.

The vile summons for him had come. He read it again, holding it with trembling hands. Sam stood by helplessly, holding his head and moaning, unable to control his terror. Jacob was the only one left for him. *I am not leaving him to these murderers,* Jacob swore.

He decided they would run; after a mad scramble to pack some things, he and Sam locked up the apartment and walked down the hall to Ruben's apartment. He answered their knock.

"Hello, boys." Tall and almost skeletal, he was fortunate to still be alive. He was a good man and a dear friend.

Jacob's throat was so tight he could hardly get the words out. "I got my summons today."

"Oh, dear God, no. I'm so sorry." Ruben's smile vanished. He reached out and put his hands on Jacob's shoulders. "God help us. Is there anything I can do?"

Jacob felt Ruben's hands trembling. He took them into his own and held them a few moments.

"Thank you for caring so much. We're going to run. I padlocked the door; can you keep the key until we get back?"

"Absolutely. I'll put it under that washtub outside my door for you when you want back in." He glanced down the hallway. "If I'm not, ah, *here* anymore, the key will still be there."

"NO! Don't say that, Ruben." Sam's tone was more animal howl than teenage boy.

"Oh, I'll be okay; don't you worry about me. I'm too tough for them." His smile reappeared, forming deep laugh lines around his eyes from all the good years.

There was no time for conversation. It was nearing sunset. The boys shook his hand, warm with friendship though frail, and left him standing there waving good-bye. Outside they faced the late afternoon sun's cold, weak light. Even the sun seemed to have lost its purpose in this nightmare.

"We have to find a warm place overnight. I wonder if Aunt Anne would take us in."

"Yeah, she'd be good. Let's go," urged Sam, shifting from one foot to the other in the below-zero weather.

When they got there, Aunt Anne answered the door, wiping her hands on her apron. As soon as she saw them, she threw her arms around them, fresh tears streaking down her face. "Oh, my dear boys."

"Auntie, how are you doing? We're so sorry about Uncle Zajdel," Jacob said. "I love him and miss him already."

"He was the light of my world," she cried, wiping tears from her face.

Maybe it was a mistake to come here; now we've upset her, thought Jacob, but Sam interrupted, in his impatience.

"Can we stay here? We're running away from the police. Kuba got his summons today."

She looked around quickly; there were no police nearby. "Come in, boys, quietly." She shut the door behind them. "Oh, my; I just don't know what to do."

The poor woman was coming undone; Jacob regretted bothering her, but then she seemed to snap out of it; she'd thought of something she could do for them.

"Are you hungry?" she asked.

"We haven't eaten, but here is some food." Jacob set the bag on the table.

"I don't need that. I have a little extra. I haven't been eating too well, you know. Grief has knocked me down to the ground."

"God can bring you back up, Auntie," said Jacob, putting his arm around her. He wasn't sure how *much* she would come back from this; she seemed in a daze and had lost quite a bit of weight since he saw her last.

"I know God can," she said. "Here, sit down while I fix something." Jacob thought that was good; at least she had some positive action to take.

While heading over to the stove she suddenly stopped like she remembered something. "Your Papa was taken, wasn't he?"

"Yes, Auntie, last year." Jacob said, the pain flooding his brain again. "We are planning to reunite after the war."

"Of course you will." She said, but her smile was uncertain. She turned to the stove.

They slept on her couch two nights. She cheered up because they had a good visit, but the morning of the third day she became agitated again.

"They're going to come shoot you. And they'll shoot me, too," she wailed, burying her face in her apron.

"No, Auntie. We'll go." Jacob said. "You have done enough; we're so grateful."

He walked over to Sam who didn't seem able to move.

"What's the matter with you?"

"Do we really have to go out there and sleep in the cold tonight?" Sam murmured.

Jacob lowered his voice. "It doesn't matter, Sam. Look at her. We have to get out of here and spare her the worry. Come on, get up."

Sam sighed and stood up. "I know we need to." He gathered up his things. "Thank you, Auntie, for everything," he called to her across the room.

"You boys wash up before you go. There are towels and washcloths over there. Stand behind that curtain, if you like. You probably won't get much chance to do that. Just be quick, though."

They got cleaned up as quickly as possible. Sam even washed his hair, doing a slam-bang job of it.

"Now you have to go out with wet hair. You'll freeze," Jacob said, frowning. He smoothed down some of Sam's wet hair sticking straight up. "Why did you wash it? Are you planning a romantic encounter of some kind?"

Sam looked astonished at the idea. "It was dirty," he commented.

Jacob chuckled to himself. Sam was 17 and definitely ripe for a girlfriend, whether he knew it or not. "Wear a warm hat, you crazy kid."

Sam dug through their stuff and pulled out a fuzzy green striped cap. They hugged their aunt good-bye; Jacob told her they would visit her after Hitler lost the war, and wished her the best. Then they left. At least they'd brought her a little cheer. He felt bad for her, but they had to keep going no matter what. He wouldn't let the murdering fiends win.

Jacob's thoughts turned to Claire once again. He had eventually shared the tragic news with Papa and Sam; Papa stared at him in mute defeat. Sam's face twisted in anger and he turned away, throwing a book across the room. Jacob hadn't realized they had gotten quite that attached to her.

He had to fight off the feelings of *what if;* what if they had married and given Papa some grandchildren and Sam some nieces and nephews? It was just talk, that was all. *What ifs* were just meaningless talk.

Now, as they walked between some buildings Jacob said "I wonder if I should have told Aunt Anne about Claire."

"Why, Kuba?"

"So she would know she wasn't alone. I lost someone I cared for very much, too. Claire and I were together almost a year," he said as he caught sight of a policeman at the end of the block. "Duck," he urged Sam.

They dropped to their knees and crawled behind a trash bin. They waited a bit and then Jacob peered around the side. There was no sight of the policeman.

"Come on, let's get away from this area," he said.

They began walking, sticking close to the buildings, trying to hide in shadows.

"I think that would just further depress her."

"What?" Jacob asked.

"If you told Aunt Anne about Claire."

"Oh, yeah. You're probably right. You know, there's no guidebook for how to act or what to say when the whole family is being systematically murdered by the Third Reich." Warm tears formed in his eyes, but he was able to shake it off for now.

They walked past some more piles of trash. "Look, Kuba. There's a packing crate. We can stay in there." He pointed to a large wooden object lying on its side in the snow.

Jacob glanced at it and began to appreciate Sam's concern about sleeping in the cold.

"Are you serious? We can't *really* sleep outside, we'll die. I am thinking of going over to Fela's house."

"Cousin Fela?" Sam liked her; she had the same name as their sister.

"Yes, come on, let's get over there. The temperature is dropping like a rock. My hands are already numb."

Sam nodded, his shiny brown hair hidden under the hat. "Mine are numb, too; let's go."

They hurried over, their noses and ears bright red by the time they got there. It was well below freezing.

She opened the door, wearing a white bathrobe and slippers. The warmth from inside spilled out to greet them. "Come in, boys. Get out of the cold." She ushered them in. "What's going on?"

"I got my Nazi 'wedding invitation'. I have to run now, because I am not getting on that train." Jacob said with emotions aflame, increased by hunger and exhaustion. "They are not going to kill me or Sam." A few tears slipped out and she embraced him.

"Of course not, Kuba," she smiled lovingly. "Come and have some dinner." She had prepared some chicken and vegetables for her midday meal. They sat down and wolfed down every bite.

"Delicious," pronounced Sam.

Cousin Fela was in her twenties and lived alone; her mother Hilda and Mama were sisters. Jacob felt his mother's presence now. She had always been so close with her family; there were seven children. Five girls and two boys. Her sister Esther had married the sock guy and was their favorite aunt, but they loved them all.

Mama's other two sisters were Ryfka and ?. Now he couldn't remember. His mind was too scattered.

They spent the afternoon on family news. Uncle Zajdel was from the other side of the family and not related to cousin Fela, but she knew him. Jacob described their stay with Aunt Anne. She was saddened to hear about Zajdel's death and also about Schmul's family. She was horrified to hear the news about Henry and their Father. She hoped that their sister Fela was all right. They all said a little prayer right then.

That evening Fela showed them where they could sleep, on a couch in the corner of her one-room apartment; they would have to share it, but they would be warm.

Two days later on Monday morning, Jacob looked outside. The day was cold and clear. Sam and he would go get their weekly rations at the store and add some food to Fela's cooking. She had a factory job, so she left them to get their own breakfast.

At the store, Jacob looked at the food on the counter. The old gentleman storekeeper had laid out some barley, dried beans, a little bread, a little apple and a small sack of sugar for each. "I wish I could give you more, boys, but if I do, others might starve. Also you know what would happen if I were caught."

"Right," said Jacob. "The same thing that always happens."

"I'm glad you understand." He lowered his voice and looked around. "Those trigger-happy bastards. Pardon my cussing."

"You can cuss Nazis all you want." Jacob assured him. "Can we eat here in the store?"

The man's face went pale. He probably guessed they were on the run, but didn't ask. It put him in danger. "Certainly boys, but make it quick, okay?"

"Thank you, sir. We will see you next week." He waved good-bye to the man and he and Sam went to a corner of the store and ate the bread and their apples. Afterwards, they left immediately.

Later that afternoon, they returned to cousin Fela's. For the evening meal they shared the barley and she had a tomato and some left-over chicken. For dessert, they put a pinch of their sugar on an apple Fela provided, and shared it.

Two more days passed. That night, the boys were resting on the couch underneath blankets when they were startled by a knock at the door.

Fela opened it a crack and signaled with her hand to remain absolutely silent. They pulled the covers over their heads.

"Hello, pretty one" said the man, as he entered. The boys heard him give her a kiss. They knew she had a boyfriend who was a Jewish policeman, but were surprised that he turned up so unexpectedly. They lay there under the blankets, afraid to breathe.

Fela and her friend talked for a little while and she told him she needed to get to sleep early. He left, finally.

"Boys, it's okay. I don't think he saw you."

"What if he saw our blankets move when we breathed?" Jacob asked. "Would he see it and maybe not say anything until he got back to work?"

"He might say he saw you on the street. I doubt he'd say anything to implicate me."

"We'll leave tomorrow morning."

"I'm sorry, Jacob. I wish I could keep you here for months."

"It's fine." Jacob gave her a hug. "We have other places to stay," he said, mustering the last drop of his courage. "Go to bed and don't worry."

Sam and Jacob stared at each other. Would the police come back tonight? They lay there, scared to move. Finally after several hours of whispers and prayers, they fell asleep.

Jacob was up at dawn. He had trouble waking Sam up, who was exhausted. "Come on, Lazybones. Get up."

Sam rolled off of the couch and rubbed his eyes. Soon they were dressed and slipped out the door, leaving a thank you note on the table for cousin Fela.

"Don't sign our names," Sam cautioned.

"Oh, yeah, you're right. The police could see that and she'd be in trouble. I'll just say 'It was nice seeing you again' and sign it *Robert* and *Alfred*.

"Good job, Alfred," Sam said.

"At your service, Robert."

⚬⚭⚬

They never saw their sweet cousin Fela again. Another bitter pill -- Aunt Anne also disappeared into the fog of the Nazi reign of terror. Nor did they see Schmul and his family after the war.

On the streets, they tried to keep moving to stay warm. They went into a few shops to get some warmth, but had to constantly watch for police. In the evening they went to another friend's house. The family was kind and let them stay several nights, though they were so crowded. The boys tried not to eat too much, because of all their children.

The second and third weeks they got the rations in the same way, and stayed with various friends. They had missed seeing David a few times when they went by his apartment; today they found him at home. His family had been leaving frequently to avoid receiving a summons. They were very nervous.

Jacob told them it wasn't that easy to outwit the Nazis, but sincerely wished them luck.

"Don't go," David said. "You can stay tonight. Then tomorrow I'll go with you."

"No, I'm a wanted man. We won't put you in that kind of danger." Jacob said. "It's all right."

"No, I insist. Get in here," he said as he grabbed the shoulder of Jacob's coat. "We'll survive." He sounded brave but Jacob knew how nervous the family was and was conflicted about staying.

"We'll only stay one night," he said. He understood the family's fear. All he had to do was think of what happened to Uncle Zajdel over a simple radio.

The next morning they left David's apartment after promising to keep in touch and walked along, talking. "I miss Papa. Mama too," Sam complained. "Oh, God, don't let this happen. Please kill Hitler. Do *something* to help us."

Kill Hitler? Jacob chuckled at Sam's prayer; God wasn't a hit man. He patted his brother's back. "We'll be okay. *God* won't kill Hitler but the Allies will."

They got up and moved down the street through an alley shadowed by tall apartment buildings. They passed by Clair's old building. In a flash Jacob was overcome with misery. He plunked down on the sidewalk once more.

"Come on, Kuba, we have to hide."

Stiff from cramped sleeping arrangements and the cold, he got back up and said "Let's go, then," stuffing away the raw pain. He'd deal with it later. *Probably for years*, he thought.

On the street they saw Abe, their casual friend from school who lost an eye during the road massacre; he had healed up. He wore a patch because they had no money for a glass eye. Jacob didn't ask to stay with them; they weren't that close. He wished him well in his recovery.

David walked up to them on the street. "There you are! Come back home with me. I've been too worried about you; I don't want you to leave yet."

It didn't take much convincing. They were happy to see David, always good for a laugh.

That night they talked about the idiocy of Hitler turning on his ally, Russia.

"What's the matter with him?" Jacob asked.

"Do you want the short answer?" David asked. "He's crazy."

"What's the long answer?" Sam asked, looking puzzled.

"He has no conscience, is some sort of mutant, self-centered and selfish to the core, pathologically hates Jews, and in World War I got shot up in his privates."

"No!" Sam's mouth dropped open four inches. "How do you know that? About the gunshot?"

"I've heard the rumor several times. He actually was blinded for three weeks once from gunshot trauma, too. That would be enough to mess you up mentally, wouldn't it?"

"Absolutely," said Jacob, "though I can't think of a more deserving person."

David's parents were starting to get nervous, and Jacob understood. They had spent two more nights there, and then returned to the street about 10:00 in the morning. David was gone on an errand.

Their feet and hands soon were frozen blocks of wood. They crawled behind things all around the ghetto. While sitting behind a barrel on some broken pieces of fencing, they talked.

"Remember, Papa always used to hold me on his lap and say 'Kuba, I'd like you to be a doctor'?" Jacob laughed.

"Yes. You're still going to be a dentist?"

"I sure am." he said, moving over to get more comfortable and stretch his legs out. "That's one of the things that keeps me going; my dream."

Sam sat up a little straighter. "Papa thought I could write books that would sell."

"If anyone can, you could. You must have read every book in the library."

Sam laughed. It was so good to see that.

Later, sneaking down a back street, they tried to step lightly to soften the crunch of their feet on the snow-packed ground. The icicles hanging off roofs were sparkly, even beautiful, but they didn't have time for art appreciation.

Three weeks of running was enough. They were out of places to hide, and Jacob felt the clock ticking, their time of freedom fading away. They were getting colder every day because of their poor diet.

It was time to go home and face whatever they had to face.

CHAPTER 15

Stolen Lives   March/1944

(8) Jews captured by Germans during the Warsaw Ghetto Uprising, April-May 1943. This photo appeared in the Stroop Report, compiled by SS Major General Juergen Stroop, commander of German forces that suppressed the uprising. Evidence at the Nuremberg trials, this photo is one of the iconographic images of the Holocaust. Josef Blösche, the Nazi with the gun, was executed in 1969.

THEY WERE HUDDLED NEXT TO a shed, taking a rest break and shivering. Sam searched Jacob's face. "Where now?"

"Sam, we can't ask these good people to keep risking their lives for us. We have to go home. Agreed?"

Sam looked at the ground, stamping a frozen foot to get some feeling in it. "Okay," he said, looking drained.

"We'll survive all this," Jacob said, more hope than fact. "Let's move on. I need to get my blood circulating."

They noticed a man curled up on the corner by a building. He was either dead or dying. "Don't look at him," said Sam, with a hard edge unusual for him. "It will make us go crazy."

"Say a prayer for him and let's just go on," said Jacob.

When they had checked with Ruben a few days earlier, he told them the thugs had come to the apartment several times, but left when they got no response.

Was it possible those hell hounds would give up?

Not likely, he thought, wishing he had a machine gun to tuck inside his coat.

As they walked down an alley, Sam asked "What did those railroad guys say again?"

"They told everybody that out of the hundreds of thousands of Jews they delivered to the camps, no one ever came back out. There was also a smell of burning flesh.'

Sam blanched.

"I'm sorry. You didn't need to hear that." Jacob mentally slapped himself.

Sam walked tall. I'm man enough."

"All right then, yes you are." Jacob gave him a little smile. "So I'll tell you. They said they suspected Jews were being *murdered* in those camps and maybe if we knew about it we could somehow save ourselves."

Sam stopped, incredulous. "Why don't the railroad men quit taking people there?"

"Because they need work to feed their families. And don't forget if the Nazis catch a whiff of anyone questioning their actions, they kill them; the workers have to act like everything is peachy. Nazis want the whole operation kept quiet; they must think people are too stupid to figure it out."

Sam blew warm breath on his hands. Jacob watched, his conscience pounding away at him. How could he drag Sam back home into mortal danger? Then he realized with a fresh jolt of misery it was life or death no matter what they did.

His head ached; he needed sleep. "I'm so tired of running, Sam, aren't you?"

Quietly Sam said "Yeah. We're doing the right thing going home."

They returned to the apartment and got the key from Ruben, who followed them back.

As he opened the padlock, feeling it click and loosen in his hand, Jacob wondered how much longer any of them would be alive. He was especially tired; he didn't usually think that way.

"Good luck, boys," Ruben said, taking the key. Worry clouded his eyes. "God be with you."

"Thank you; and God provide for you, too," Jacob said, shaking his hand. They crept like burglars into their own apartment. No point in advertising their presence.

"I'll walk by regularly and sing something; if you need anything or want to leave come to the door and knock on it. Don't be afraid it's the police. They don't sing."

Jacob chuckled.

Ruben stopped a moment and glanced down the hall. He drew a deep breath. He looked sad to say good-bye. With a little wave, he shut the door, locking it up again.

"I've heard there is no escape from Nazi law. The odds are something terrible," Sam said, rubbing his hands briskly.

"It's okay, I'll think of something." Jacob glanced through the window. Was God listening? He saw no sign in the heavens; nothing but the grey sky of late afternoon, herding its fat charcoal clouds around like a mother bear with her cubs. It was going to drop a load of snow on them soon.

Five minutes later a sharp knock rattled the door. The boys turned white and ran over into the corner of the room. *They're here already?*

Then they heard David's voice. "Kuba, are you in there?"

Jacob went to the door. "Go next door and get Ruben to let you in, but be quiet."

Shortly David was back, and came in to join them. Ruben waved at them, locked the door again and left.

"You left without saying good bye. How is it going?" David asked.

"We're sorry we missed you that morning, but your mother was worried. There's been no sign of the police yet, but we've only been here a few hours."

"How soon do you think they'll come?"

"I don't know. It's been three weeks. They've been here a couple times and left."

"Oh, they'll give up, then. They don't pay them enough to make that big an effort," David said, hatred coloring his voice.

"I'm not so sure; this is life or death for them, too," said Jacob.

"How soon will they come?" asked Sam, his face a mask of horror.

"Keep your voices down," Jacob whispered sharply.

"Don't be all grouchy with *us*," complained Sam. "This isn't our fault."

Jacob put his hand on Sam's shoulder and took a deep, calming breath. "I'm sorry, I'm just so nervous. Let's sit down in that straw and try to relax. You want to stay, David? I can't guarantee they will leave you alone if they come, and there's not much to eat. You'll have to stay at least until Ruben comes to check on us; we're locked in."

"After you left this morning I had a feeling it was so final. I'll stay a while and keep you company; then I'll go. I wanted to spend some time together before, I mean, *IF* any of us has to leave."

"You're a good friend," Jacob said, hugging him, then arranged some straw on the floor away from the window so they wouldn't be seen.

The boys crawled onto it with a blanket. It was scratchy, but they hardly noticed. It was twenty below zero outside, and inside as well. Ice crystals were forming inside the windows from the moisture in the boys' breathing. The room seemed almost like a living thing, fighting the cold along with them, as frosty crystals twinkled in the window.

Unfortunately, there was no time left to enjoy the small wonders in life. Jacob and Sam sat there like condemned prisoners, their faces masks of tragedy. David didn't look much happier. Jacob rubbed his tingling legs, starting to burn as they warmed up a degree or two. At least they were sheltered from the wind.

"Should I do my Goebbels walk?" David teased, a feeble effort to cheer them up.

"No, I don't think this would be the time," Jacob said, smiling at the memory.

They made some small talk, then all dozed off.

Jacob dreamed fitfully of running free through a field with a faceless figure pursuing him. He was a fighter. His subconscious was already churning out alternative plans while he slept.

He rolled over again and now he was too cold to sleep. His thoughts were of Mama. He looked around at the dreary little one-room apartment. *Thank God Mama never had to live here. She would have been so heartbroken to lose her lovely home.*

Then he remembered the way she put her arms around all four of her children at once. "You are my most precious possessions," she always said. None of this material stuff would have mattered. *She is an angel,* he thought. *Right now she is singing in some choir with the angels and looking down on us.*

He finally fell asleep and dozed on and off. Sam was so exhausted and emotionally spent he slept like a rock. David was also sleeping.

In the 2:00 a.m. darkness they were startled by footsteps and conversation outside in the hallway.

The police.

Sam sat up. He looked at Jacob with big, wide eyes. His words came in a rush. *"Kuba, our whole family is gone and I've decided I don't want to stay here alone. Where you go, I go. Whatever happens to you, happens to me."* He was gripping his brother's arm so tightly it hurt.

Confronted by this terrible choice, Jacob recoiled like someone punched him hard in the stomach, but he pulled himself together and hugged sweet, trusting Sam tightly to himself.

"I'd be glad to have you with me, but I don't want you hurt. You're so young and intelligent. You have a brilliant future. Getting on that train means death. Do you really understand that?"

"I don't care. I won't stay here and die alone." Sam buried his face in his hands, sobbing now.

Jacob hugged Sam's face to him, to stifle the noise. He tried to reassure him with the hug.

David woke up, rubbing his eyes. "Are you okay?"

"Noises outside. Stay away from the window," Jacob whispered. Then he sat back and stared at Sam. What was he supposed to do? Once again, there was no guide book. He couldn't even imagine Sam coping with Nazis by himself. Even if Sam stayed with David, there might be a day when David had to leave him.

Jacob had no way to stop this tragedy barreling through their lives like one of those damn Nazi trains, and miracles were far too scarce around there. So Sam would stay with him; there wasn't any time to talk about it, anyway.

Now the police boots shuffled at the door. Frustrated by the padlock, the thugs discussed leaving it alone, while the boys' lives hung in the balance; two minutes, two centuries long.

"What should I do?" gasped David. "Will they take me?"

Jacob put his finger to his lips. "I don't know, but I'll explain you weren't summoned," he whispered.

Outside a deep voice said "Oh, *this* place. We were here before, remember? They're probably dead by now. Let's move on."

"*No!* They could still be in there." The higher voice urged.

"All right, then; go ahead and kick in the door," said the first one.

Sam's rapid breathing and sheen of sweat in this arctic cold made his terror plain to see. Jacob could almost feel it coming from him. He stroked Sam's back, hoping to calm him. Helping Sam strengthened him, too.

"It will be okay," he whispered to David and Sam.

In the hall, the higher voice took on an edge. "What are you going to do? Stand there and watch? That's a lot of work. It's the middle of the night and I'm tired and too damn cold. What the hell; you're right. Let's just go."

There was a deep, mumbled reply. The higher voice answered, "So you're feeling guilty now? Don't worry about the captain; he won't know. They weren't here, that's all."

Jacob stopped breathing for a bit, pulse hammering in his ears. Was this their miracle?

He grabbed Sam's hand and squeezed it. "See, God will take care of us," he whispered, brushing a tear from Sam's eye. Sam nodded, but turned his head to the wall, whispering soft little prayers of his own.

Please go away, Jacob begged silently. *Please, please.*

David began pacing. *"Bastards," he muttered.*

"Please sit down" Jacob whispered. "They might hear you."

The lower-voiced one out in the hall sounded alarmed. "Look, you lazy lout, we can't just ignore orders. You know very well what will happen if we're caught. We'll be on that train. You're the one who thinks they're in there. Let's go get a crowbar."

Noooo. Jacob thought. *Please, no.* David jumped up and started pacing again.

More clunking of boots down the hall; the sound gradually faded away.

"Are they leaving?" Sam asked, saucer-eyed.

Jacob shrugged his shoulders and again signaled them to stay quiet. He strained to hear. Everything depended on whether the police resolved their differences and found a crowbar. Jacob hated those evil things. On the streets, the Jew-hater's weapon of choice.

Soon deep laughter boomed out on the dark street, one of them enjoying himself.

How can he? Doesn't he know how this is going to end? What is funny? How can these Jewish police round up their own kind like this? Sure, they're afraid of the train, but I'd find another line of work if I were them. Or starve.

Jacob pressed his eyes with his fingers and tried to come up with the right prayer that God would hear. No human plan was going to do a thing for them now.

"Come on, Kuba, let's get out of here," Sam begged.

"We can't just run out into the darkness; our bodies are so broken down we'll die from the cold. Besides, we're locked in, remember?"

As the seconds ticked by, they fell into grim silence. He thought about Fela. Was she alive? Was Papa? And Henry? The grief almost smothered him. He felt short of breath and wished he had an oxygen tank and could just lie there and breathe from it. *Mama, please help us,* he muttered.

The sound of boots coming down the hall filled them with dread. Jacob desperately wanted to stay in control for Sam's sake, but he could only watch his body jerk and tremble. It was making the decisions now, not him.

Then he heard Sam softly crying into the blanket. Once more, strength from within found its way to the surface and answered the call. He took Sam by the shoulders.

"Don't give up. It may look bad right now but I'll take care of us both. I really will." It was a brave piece of acting, one that he only partially believed, but he wouldn't tell Sam that. Sam leaned against him and clung tightly. David sat down and hugged them, saying "God help us."

The boots were at the door again. There was movement out in the hall. A *crack;* the door flew open and two dark figures materialized. All three boys shrank back. The police came forward, reaching out with one hand and holding a baton in the other.

"Which one of you is Jacob Eisenbach?" They were all business.

"I am, and he is a friend, David. Don't take him, he hasn't been summoned."

David started quaking.

The policeman looked at David. "You. Get out."

"Good-bye, Kuba and Sam," David said as he ran out the door.

"Come on, then, get up. You have to go," the deeper-voiced one said. He was a good-sized man. He really didn't need to wave that baton around.

"Don't beat us; we'll go," Jacob said. Then he put his arm around Sam. "He's coming with me," he said, in as firm a manner as he could muster. He didn't want any flak about that.

The police apparently didn't care one way or the other. "Get up," they said again.

The boys stood up slowly. Jacob's legs were cramping. Poor, frightened Sam was almost glued to his side as they moved toward the door, police behind them.

Mama, be with us, Jacob whispered, as he and Sam stumbled out into the hall. They were herded into the night with no idea what tomorrow would hold.

The boys never saw David or their neighbor Ruben again.

CHAPTER 16

A Ride On Satan's Train   March/1944

(9) The famous entrance to Auschwitz. 'Arbeit Macht Frei' means 'Work Makes You Free'. Quite an insult. Young Henry was brought here from the hospital to be gassed, with no family accompanying him.

THEY MADE THE BOYS WALK a long way to the train station in that bitter cold, their feet and hands numb as bricks. Their brains were frozen too. They glanced around for a sign of someone watching, someone who might help them. No one did; if they tried, they'd have been arrested or just murdered outright.

They were in a dark, heartless place, nothing like the world they were born into.

How can your life just turn itself inside out and become some hellish place you don't even recognize? Jacob wondered.

They walked close together, trying to capture some warmth. Sam was quiet. Jacob thought about Mama. Was she watching this? He asked her again to help them if she could. It felt like no one on earth cared, but wherever they went, at least the boys would be together.

Where you go, I go. Jacob thought about Sam's words and was determined to protect him, whatever it took. He would *not* let the Nazis hurt Sam. They both would survive this.

At the train station Jews were milling around in groups, some trying to reassure each other, others in stony silence. Armed soldiers stood around. The boys stared at the big boxcars. Was this their death, then? Though nothing could surprise them anymore, this would be one of the worst experiences they endured.

They joined a group of equally frightened Jews waiting to board. Sam and he huddled close, to support each other emotionally and share some warmth.

Jacob thought again of poor sick Henry, taken from the hospital to the gas chamber – piled in the back of a truck - with no family to comfort him as he entered the 'shower'. By now, they knew more details about the gas chambers.

Those vicious Nazis have no souls, or they could never have done what they did to Henry, he thought. The memory was almost physically painful.

When enough people had been rounded up, they were ordered into a car. On the way to it, soldiers handed each person a bottle of water and a small loaf of bread. This was the 'meal' promised to Jews if they showed up for boarding.

Sometimes Nazis kicked people to make them hurry, while other soldiers stood by and laughed. They took people's baggage and said it would be sent to their new location. The boys had no luggage with them; they were wearing three layers of clothing they had been wearing when picked up, but the hell hounds didn't notice or didn't care.

It was their turn to climb on board. Would they even survive this ride? Jacob couldn't think about it now; he had to focus on one minute at a time. To do otherwise would have shattered him mentally. Jacob went first, then reached a hand down to help Sam up.

Inside the car, people were packed so tightly there was no room to sit down. They stood together, waiting. Jacob's heart pounded against his chest like it was trying to escape the Nazis on its own. The big door rolled shut and was latched.

Soon the wheels screeched and the train jerked forward. It finally began to roll. As it chugged forward without mercy, people were screaming and crying, making the suffering worse. It was an all-male group, but some were crying like young girls as the wheels picked up speed. Some of them started losing their minds; others collapsed and spouted gibberish until they ran out of steam.

"Marie!" called out one. "My Marie, where are you?" He sobbed and wailed as if his heart was breaking and each sharp piece was cutting him inside.

There was a silent passenger in the car: *Death*. Fear chilled their every breath as the terrible train chugged along toward the killing place.

They expected to arrive at the death camp anytime soon. The brothers dozed a few minutes standing up and packed tightly between people. It was impossible to sleep for long, rolling toward the gas chamber. They suffered physically, but emotionally it was sheer torture.

The car was closed up with little air getting in. There were no bathroom stops, so the Nazis thoughtfully provided a bucket in the car. Jacob remarked "Animals are cared for better than this," to no one in particular, and no one replied; each passenger was intent on his own survival.

There were a couple of tiny windows, but they couldn't see the guards. They needn't have wondered; they were there. They had a little place to sit outside of the car.

As they bumped along, the screaming raked the boys' nerves raw and made the ride excruciating. High-pitched screams, low keening moans, prayers, crying, but no conversation. The ones not screaming stood there like mannequins, until someone fell over and died. The bodies were all over the floor where they fell between people. Hands reached out to take their bread or water if there was any left.

They didn't arrive soon, like they thought; they spent three days in that rolling hell. Hours passed while army trains went by. *These monsters deserve to die for this one trip alone,* Jacob thought. His stomach ached with hunger. His back hurt; he longed to lie down and sleep.

Because he was so weak, he worried he would pass out and be left for dead, or whatever they did with corpses. He couldn't think about that now. He went through some prayers he had memorized from childhood.

Sometimes he worried he'd snap and grab a gun or attack a soldier before he could get his reason back; then, of course, would come his death. Probably a very painful one. *Please God, don't let me do that; Sam would be left alone.*

Finally the train pulled into a station. They had arrived at what they believed was their final destination. For many, it was.

"Get out, you dirty Jews!"

Jacob grabbed Sam's hand and pulled him through the pile of bodies, hoping they could find a chance to take off running without guns pointing at them. They jumped down from the train and were blinded by the sun, reflecting off the snow blanketing the ground.

Shading his eyes, Jacob saw big, frightening SS officers milling around. One of them looked right at him; his eyes scanned him and Sam; a predator sizing up his prey. Jacob wished he'd never been born. He now says if it were possible to die from terror, that would have been his end right there.

He looked over at Sam, who was staring up at the SS officer, open-mouthed. The officer turned away.

"Are you sorry you came with me?" Jacob asked.

"No, Kuba; it's my destiny to be with you to the end."

Jacob gazed at him. *What can I say to that?* "God bless you, Sam. You're so special." He smiled and hugged his brother. "You're being so strong after all this; I'm proud of you."

Sam gave him a wan little smile.

Jacob looked around the group of surviving Jews; everyone looked dazed and exhausted, like he was. One man moaned to no one in particular "Let my death be quick; I can't bear the waiting anymore." A few minutes later he said it again, and kept repeating it. He sank to his knees and asked God to take him.

Jacob just shook his head. *Poor soul; you better stop that, or the Nazis will grant your wish.*

He now spoke to God. *Thank you for the strength you have given me. Help me to face what's coming bravely, and help me take care of Sam.*

CHAPTER 17

A Stay Of Execution   3/1944

(10) Hungarian Jews on their way to die. What was their crime?

IN MAY, 1944 THE HUNGARIAN Jews pictured above had newly arrived at Auschwitz, unaware they would shortly be in Gas Chamber and Crematorium #1. In that one room 60,000 Jews were gassed. Murder was done in two 12-hour shifts round the clock.

As for Sam and Jacob, they could breathe again. They were not at Auschwitz, but at the labor camp of Skarzysko with an ammunition factory where they would work. They shivered with relief at this news. This would save some, but not all of their lives.

Jacob, like everyone, hoped that Hitler would take on something too big and stumble, and that wish was granted. Hitler had attacked Russia, his own ally; it was a country far too big and cold to invade in wintertime. It would eventually bring about the end of Adolf's grisly moment in the sun.

After the freezing Battle of Stalingrad in Russia devastated Hitler's army, he took Germans out of factories and sent them to the Russian front. Unlike the Allies, he did not put women to work for the war effort. He used the Jewish prisoners instead; that bought the prisoners some precious time.

But there was still the sorting of workers to go through at the train station, *the selection committee.* They lined up and a tall, muscle-bound SS officer in black uniform and skull-and-crossbones hat eyed each one as they trembled toward him. He ordered them either left or right. He didn't say, but he was handing out death sentences.

Jacob and Sam had some friends from home in their group which was sent to the right. They seemed to be healthier than the other group.

"Kuba, look!"

"What?"

"Ben is over there."

Jacob could hardly believe it. Ben was in their group! They waved at each other across the large group of people.

Jacob and Sam hurried over to him. "You came on the same train as we did?"

"I must have. We didn't get a formal summons. Some friends and I were just rounded up off the street. I don't even know where one of them is, and the other one died on the train."

"I'm so sorry." Jacob said.

Ben nodded at him. "I just hope my family is okay. I haven't seen any of them."

"We will pray for them. Imagine; we were destined to go through this together. We'll help each other survive. I know it's going to be okay, Ben."

They caught sight of another friend of theirs, Srul, standing in front of the big, frightening SS officer. He was directed to go into the weaker, sicklier group on the left. Realizing he was in grave danger, he stood with tears running down his face, seemingly unable to move. They shoved him over into his group, adding a whack of the baton on his back. He stood there, tears streaming, and shifted one foot to the other. He looked ready to explode. Jacob shared his terror and prayed. *Please, God, help him; help us all.*

Finally Srul found the courage and made a rare and bold move; he slipped out of his group and snuck around to join Jacob and Sam. Just one glance, one turn of an officer's head, and he would have had bullets rip through him. Jacob and Sam might have gone down with him if the officer's aim was careless.

They never knew from minute to minute when their lives would be snuffed out. Fortunately Srul survived the selection and later worked with them in the factory.

They were in group 'A' assigned to work at precision grinding machines making bullet shells.

Imagine me making bullets so they can kill Jews, Jacob muttered to himself. *Oh God, please wake me from this nightmare.*

They would have work stations and do 12-hour shifts on little food. Group 'B' would do the same work as Group 'A'; another group had the terrible luck to be put in Group 'C', which was doomed. Groups A and B would send them the bullet shells and Group C would fill them with a poisonous substance. The Nazis wanted a few months of work from them before they died. They would get no protective clothes and would do 12-hour days. People in group C would turn yellow as a taxi cab and die in three to six months.

Replacements were no problem.

In Nazi camps, people were forced to work until they collapsed. Once they couldn't work anymore, if they didn't oblige the Nazis by dying they were beaten to death, shot or gassed.

The Jewish Chief back in the Ghetto, Chaim Rumkowski, was a weighty man with a big voice. Before the war he was the director of an orphanage; the Nazis thought he'd be a good leader. They forced him to round up 600 to 10,000 Jews for each run, using the Jewish police. He fulfilled their expectations perfectly.

Jacob doesn't hold anything against him. Rumkowski said if he cooperated it might pacify the Nazis and they wouldn't come in and massacre everyone like they did other places.

He fatally underestimated the Nazis.

A few months after Jacob and Sam were taken on the train, Heinrich Himmler 'liquidated' the ghetto, sending everyone but a few hundred to the gas chamber. The remaining Jews were left to close up and try to destroy evidence, under supervision, of course. If Sam and Jacob had not been forced to go in March, they would have died during this liquidation. Jacob didn't know it at the time, but his 'wedding invitation' saved their lives.

One day not too long after Jacob and Sam left, Rumkowski looked up from his desk to see Hitler's goons staring at him. He tried to remain calm, but they made quick work of dragging him out, refusing to answer his questions. One can imagine his cries and begging.

"Wait a minute! I'm *Chief of the ghetto;* I do a great service for you. No, Wait! Himmler needs me to run everything. Please, listen to me."

He was wrong about that; they were liquidating this ghetto and didn't need him at all. They ignored him and tossed him into the group boarding the train. His family went on the same train. It is unknown whether he saw them.

A few agonizing days later, Rumkowski stumbled out of the boxcar in shock. He had been standing for three days, watching people die in front of him, and trying to move aside as they fell. On arriving at Auschwitz, he soon found himself in the gas chamber, staring at those nozzles along with other Jews from his ghetto.

Before entering the gas chamber, he would have seen prisoners forced to help the disabled people and young children undress. The prisoner-helpers' pathetic faces showed their agony at having to do this.

In a post-war interview, one of them described how he made a point to always go into the 'shower' with a group to keep them calm. At the last minute, he left, and the door was sealed shut. He would be crushed with guilt every time. One of the more fiendish ways the Nazis tortured people was making them participate in the destruction of their fellow Jews.

Jacob knew he was fortunate to have survived so far. Still he didn't have any peace of mind. Like everyone else he was tormented by the thought *When will it be my turn? Is today the day they'll torture me to death?*

CHAPTER 18

The Nightmare Of Skarzysko   MARCH 1 1944 - JULY 1 1944

(11) <u>Dachau: Inspection by the Nazi party, 5/8/36</u>. This is Heinrich Himmler, strutting peacock, head of the SS core of assassins, a brutal and purposely terrifying man. People say he resembled a rat. Being face to face with Himmler must have felt like death was breathing down this prisoner's neck.

JACOB AND SAM WALKED INTO the barracks; he was not surprised to see the colorless, dreary walls and sad faces. There were three layers of hard bunks with straw 'mattresses' full of bedbugs and lice. To his utter disgust, he would soon find he could feel them crawling on him.

Since he and Sam wore several layers of clothes when captured, they could change clothes and wash them in the barracks. They had showers, but no hot water. Unfortunately, it didn't solve the bug problem.

Sam's shoes were worn out, so he was issued a pair of wooden shoes. They weren't much good for walking any distance and they were freezing cold in the winter weather, so he wrapped rags around his feet in place of socks. Jacob's shoes were in better condition so he didn't need wooden ones.

Jacob, enterprising as always, managed to find people who had extra rations and traded clothes for food. A pair of socks would bring enough food to last several weeks. He made a new friend who was assigned to work in a bakery on the *outside*, highly unusual. He was sneaking in food. What a courageous soul; if caught he'd have been tortured and killed. He traded with Jacob, who shared everything with Sam.

He and Sam kept it to themselves that they were brothers, only telling their closest friends. If the Nazis found out, they would split them up, because family provided emotional support. Nazis wanted none of that; they were out to destroy these poor people, physically and mentally.

Some more luck for the brothers: this wasn't a death camp as such, meaning gas chambers, although plenty of unfortunate prisoners died there. They weren't given tattoos nor did Nazis shave their heads or make them wear striped uniforms. Their clothes and hair were an important piece of their identity.

At lunchtime in the kitchen prisoners stood in line with their bowl for the thin turnip soup.

"Look, Kuba. I have a potato in my soup. I'll share it with you."

"You don't have to do that, Sam. I'm strong."

"No, I'll share it."

"Are you sure? There won't be any supper tonight, you know. Nothing till tomorrow morning."

"I *know,* Jacob. Remember '*Where you go, I go?*' Well, what I eat, you eat."

Jacob chuckled. "You're funny, and I love you for it."

Sam grinned. "Happy to hear it. You better love me, or I am lost."

Jacob didn't know whether that was a joke or what. "Don't worry, Sam, I'll always be here for you."

Even though they were making ammunition for the Nazis, prisoner well-being was of no importance. They did give them some bread now and then. It was a blessing, as they would have died without it.

Ben had been assigned to their barracks.

"We're neighbors in the factory too, you know. You're in the center, not too far from where I work, left of the back door. I could sneak out if I wanted," Ben bragged.

"Nice to know. Have you seen Srul around here?"

"Yes, he's in the last barracks. He works near me over by the factory door. We talk about running away."

Jacob laughed. "And where do you suppose you would go?"

"I don't know. Switzerland," he chuckled. "Remember us talking about it? Do you ever wish we had tried to escape the ghetto?"

"No, I don't. My body is still relatively free of bullet holes."

Ben laughed. "Keep on making us laugh in this place, will you?"

"Next time our work section throws a party, I'll invite you," said Jacob.

"Are you having a bad day or something?"

"No more than usual, but last night when the kapo was beating a guy who bunks next to me it made me furious. I can't believe those bastard kapos turn on fellow Jews like that."

Ben agreed. "They are slime, not human beings, just like the Nazis."

"Imagine selling out to the Nazis just for some extra food and better sleeping quarters. Be careful, Ben. They can turn you in for some stupid offense."

"And then it's *Good night, nurse,*" said Ben. "I'm aware of it. Everyone is terrified of them."

Jacob kept his bowl by his side always, at work or in the barracks. He slept with it next to his pillow. Anything to do with food was life or death.

"Why do they give us Sundays off?" asked Ben one day, as he dealt the cards.

"Probably to give factory supervisors the day off. Believe me, it's not for *our* benefit." Jacob said.

"If only we had some music," said Ben, arranging his cards. "I guess we could always sing."

"*I* could sing," commented Jacob, "but *you* are questionable." They laughed and made the best of it, trying to forget the outrageous injustice being done to them. Until the next atrocity happened, anyway.

One morning at daily roll call, the weather was freezing. The prisoners wore thin clothes; many were wearing wooden shoes and no socks, including Sam, who stood shivering.

"Why do they take so long?" Sam asked, shifting one foot to the other. "This is ridiculous."

"They enjoy torturing us," Jacob replied, feeling the anger heat up his face. If only it would heat up his whole body.

Finally the order was given to march to the factory. By this time, their feet were frozen and walking was difficult.

"Stay in line!" the guard barked at Sam, who had slowed down due to his merciless shoes.

He jumped back into line, wincing in pain.

"Be careful, Sam. Don't draw attention to yourself."

"I know, but my feet hurt so much."

"We'll be there in a minute," Jacob said. "Hang on. Grit your teeth and stare straight ahead."

When they got to the factory and stepped inside, they were greeted with some blessed warmth. Sam stopped walking to rub his feet. A guard came over and shoved him forward. "Keep moving!"

"Sam, you *must* stop making yourself obvious. Try to blend in."

"My feet are killing me. You try walking in those wooden shoes."

"This is life or death, Sam; *please* remember that."

"Don't worry; I won't mistake this for summer camp."

"Watch out, the boy has teeth!" Jacob quipped.

Jacob still had ulcers on his legs from starvation, but did not ask for help. They didn't dare go to the camp hospital; that was a place of no return.

Every Sunday the commander entered the hospital with his big German Shepherd. Jacob, Sam and Ben walked by once and observed him through an open door.

The man sauntered down the aisle, appraising the patients. Hmmm. There was one who didn't pass muster; too sick. He lifted his gun and blasted the poor man, then beamed, like he was proud of his marksmanship. Then on to the next patient who shrank back, his blanket pulled up to his eyes. He was lucky; somehow he made the grade. On to the next.

The boys were outraged, but not surprised.

After the war, at least one honcho from their camp was sentenced to death. When Jacob heard that, he hoped it was this commander.

Terrible epidemics swept through the camp, like they didn't have enough to worry about. His luck held up: he didn't come down with anything, and neither did Sam or Irene {Jacob's future wife}, or any of his friends. If they had taken Sam away from Jacob, one or both of them might have weakened considerably. The emotional support was critical.

"How do you do it, man?" asked Ben one evening in the barracks.

"What?" said Jacob.

"Keep that positive outlook all the time."

"For some reason I can make and keep friends easily, no matter how bad things get. Spending time with them, sharing our common suffering; I think that keeps me on track."

"We've all had such god-awful losses."

"Exactly," said Jacob. "There's the key."

Their camp was all Jewish; no criminals, blacks, homosexuals, Jehovah's Witnesses, Gypsies (Romanis) or other types of condemned people. They were eliminated and not used in these factories.

Guards constantly called prisoners 'dirty Jews'. No matter how often he saw cruelty, Jacob never got used to it. He's heard of some kindnesses by the officers, but he never saw it.

One Sunday Sam was sitting on his bed looking glum.

"What's wrong, old boy?" Jacob teased.

"I feel hopeless today, Kuba. That fat guard yelled at me earlier."

"What did you do wrong?"

"Some stupid minor thing. I got in his way or something. "Staying alive isn't worth it, you know? Without human dignity."

"No, no. That's the *wrong* way to think. Are you going to die today? I don't think so. Don't worry about trivial things. We're going to get out of here and throw a big party one day."

"I guess you're right. How do you stay so cheery?"

"I just had this conversation with Ben. I do it through friends."

Sam still looked distressed. Jacob pulled up a wooden crate from nearby and sat on it. "Here's the way it is, Sam. God has a plan for all of us. He wants us to trust Him and get through this a day at a time, like a test, I think. Then later we'll be rewarded with freedom and a happy life. Meanwhile He has provided us with friends. We have an opportunity to help *them* as well. That's probably the most rewarding part, helping others."

"How do you know all this?" Sam looked doubtful.

"I'm older and wiser; look at it this way. I have more experience with God." Jacob chuckled. "Let me see a smile."

Sam gave him a small smile and reached out his hand.

They shook hands. "That's my boy, Sam. If you stay positive and focus on others, you'll live longer; you'll avoid calling attention to yourself and that is worth everything. You don't dare have a Nazi think you are unstable or too sick. They'll kill you."

Sam lay back on his bed and studied the ceiling. "Kuba? Is Mama watching this?"

"Absolutely. She sends her love and strength to us every day. Can't you feel it?"

"I think so, some times."

"I definitely do. I'm going to a poetry reading right now. You should join us." It was a Sunday off; not a time to be gloomy.

Sam stood up. "All right, I'll come. It's better than hanging around here."

"Attaboy!" Jacob said.

"Why is your jaw swollen like that?"

"Don't remind me. I have to have some wisdom teeth pulled. I'm trying to get myself ready to go through it without anesthesia. They keep getting worse. The puffiness ruins my good looks, and I can't have *that.*"

Sam smiled. "Kuba, you're one of a kind. When are you going? Will you be all right?"

"Soon, from the feel of it, and yes, I'll survive it."

"If anything happens to you, Kuba -- "

"It will turn out all right. Like Papa used to say, don't borrow trouble. And if you do borrow it, return it as quickly as possible," chuckled Jacob.

"I don't have to borrow it; they dumped it on us."

Jacob sighed and shook his head. *Oh, Sam.*

"Come on, get up. Let's go join the others and hear some poetry or play cards. Let's not mope around here. Trouble will definitely find you if you sit around waiting for it."

"All right," Sam said. "You're older and wiser."

"You can only say I'm *older* until I reach a certain age you know; then it's an insult," laughed Jacob.

A few days later he saw the dentist, a fellow prisoner, a young man. He extracted the teeth and it was miserably painful, but Jacob just gripped the arms of the chair and got through it. At least the man did it quickly and did good work.

Afterward Jacob had to go right back to work. A tooth extraction didn't bleed much and he could blend right in again. For once he was glad the food was soup.

They had only a few children in the camp, mostly 12 – 15 years old. These pathetic souls stood at the fence staring out at freedom. Or they would sit on the ground and draw pictures in the dirt. Children not gassed on arrival were routinely separated from their mothers.

There were no restrictions on what officers and guards could do to prisoners. Often when Germany lost a battle (prisoners figured this out), officers came in and grabbed several people out of their chairs. The terror on their faces was heartbreaking.

Everyone knew what was coming; the officers took them upstairs to the torture room. The randomness of their selections was devastating. It could be anybody, anytime. There was almost nothing Jews could do to make themselves valuable enough for the Germans to keep them alive. Only the factory work, which they tried to do efficiently.

Jacob and his coworkers heard terrible screams from upstairs. It was nearly impossible to keep working through it, but the eyes of the German supervisors roamed up and down the row of workers, never letting up. Under their intense stares, one had to keep his head down and continue.

Later the officers carried out the bodies on stretchers, covered with bloody blankets. Jacob thought it was because the sight was too gruesome. Normally they didn't worry about prisoner sensibilities, but for this kind of murder, maybe they were afraid of a riot.

And they were nearly right, because Jacob was outraged like everyone else. His anger hammered at him over and over, but each time he had to stuff it down for survival.

These deaths still had to be reported to the Security Police. Later it was discovered they were routinely labeled as 'suicide', 'accidental death', prisoner 'trying to escape', 'assaulting a guard, or 'sabotaging production'.

Every day Jacob thought about Papa and wondered if he had been beaten and tortured. And his sister, what happened to her? Henry was probably spared all that and gassed immediately. Like everyone else, Jacob dreamed of revenge. His outrage was becoming explosive.

He fantasized killing Germans, regularly. He would use a gun, ideally a machine gun. He would line them all up by a ditch and tell them they were going to fall where there was still Jewish blood. They could mingle with *that* for a while. He relished the thought: he'd shoot them in the groin which would be painful and take a while to kill them.

No one escaped the camp. People got away with very little. It's a miracle that Srul managed to switch lines that day at the gate.

To make sure it didn't slip their minds that their fate was in Nazi hands, prisoners were forced to watch executions. They were never told what the victims did wrong. Prisoners had to watch as they strung men and women up. The gallows structure was on a platform; the condemned stood on a table with their hands tied and a rope around their necks.

Jacob stared at their frozen, dazed expressions and wondered what it felt like to be seconds from death. He prayed *Give them strength. Help them through this.* Nazis wanted it burned into prisoners' minds that this could happen to them. The gesture hit its mark; everyone was reeling with fright.

Then the beasts kicked away the table and the poor victims were left swinging and jerking while they strangled to death. Their faces turned red and bloated, while they struggled for several minutes. Some lost control of their bladders and bowels.

When they stopped wriggling, it was a relief to the unwilling observers; Jacob had cringed and unconsciously stopped breathing at times during the process. A prisoner didn't dare cover his eyes or he might be the next victim. At minimum, he would be beaten ferociously.

Every day Jacob and Sam prayed together and Jacob helped Sam focus on living one more day. They told each other, *After the war we'll be grateful and enjoy our family for the rest of our lives.*

Sam said, "I wonder what happened to Aunt Esther? I remember those great muffins she made."

"I know, Sam. We'll find everybody after the war. I know she told her kids to stay together."[3]

In the camp they could not send or receive letters. There was no communication with the outside world. No newspapers or radios.

There was still reason to hope for freedom.

The first day they heard the distant thunder of artillery, they wondered what it meant. It could be anything, but they hoped it was the Russians or Americans coming to get them. New arrivals at camp confirmed that Russia, no longer Hitler's ally, was fighting its way across Poland, defeating the Nazis.

The noise continued day and night, getting louder and louder. Judging by the nervousness of the guards, they surmised correctly that it was bad news for Germany; the rescue of the Jews was coming.

Each day it was louder; their hopes climbed. Meanwhile, what if the Nazis decided to eliminate all of them before the Allies got there?

They didn't know it, but that is exactly what the Nazis had in mind.

---

3 It later came to light that Aunt Esther died in a gas chamber. Her three sons survived the war and stayed together. They went to Australia in 1950. Their sisters apparently died in a gas chamber.

CHAPTER 19

Irene   MARCH / 1944 _ JANUARY / 1945

Irene, young wife and mother
(Dr. Eisenbach's collection)

SHE WAS STANDING IN FRONT of the ladies' bathroom in the factory hall-way. She had beautiful dark hair, chocolate brown eyes and the fairest skin he'd ever seen. Jacob had passed by her many times and tried to catch her eye by walking a little more jauntily, smiling at her. She usually turned her gaze away as he neared.

This is starting to feel like Papa's story when he met Mama, he thought. *Time for a change.*

This time he walked up to her, bold as the cockiest rooster, and introduced himself. To his delight, she responded flirtatiously.

"I'm Irene; I'm glad to meet you."

"Nice accommodations, huh?" he said, ignoring the butterflies doing handsprings in his stomach.

"First class." She asked how long he'd been there and they traded small talk for a little while.

"Maybe sometime we can eat lunch together if our groups go at the same time," he said.

"I'd like that." Her smile was so warm, Jacob thrilled to it. Then they had to get back to work.

He watched her walk towards her work station, long legs moving with a sensuous rhythm. He could get used to this.

"Wow," said Ben, who had been watching nearby. "Smooth move, my friend. Do you think she has a sister or a friend for me?"

"I don't know, buddy. I'll ask her when I get a chance."

"Who would have thought you'd find romance in a concentration camp?"

"It seems I can find it anywhere," chuckled Jacob. "I enjoy chatting with girls and they like it. You could do it, too, you know."

"I'm a little shy. I'll have to observe you more closely."

"No magic, Ben. Just be open and friendly; be interested in what *they* do instead of talking about what you do."

"What could they possibly do to be so interesting? I don't care about housekeeping and babies and clothes and female gossip."

"If they don't have thoughts and ideas that interest you, you're with the wrong girl; unless, of course, they only want to talk about *you*. Is that what you're looking for?"

"Who, me? That much of an egotist? Nah."

Jacob laughed. They went back to their work, full of wonder about what unexpected delights could possibly be hiding in a terrible place like this.

That night in the barracks, Jacob told Sam. "I've met someone special."

"Like a girl?" Sam was incredulous. "Here?"

"Yes, girls come here, too, you know."

"I know, but who thinks about that type of stuff in this place?"

"Apparently *I* do. Tell me, Sam, if you had a shot, wouldn't you take it? I mean even *here?*"

"Well, if you put it that way. . ."

"Good. Now you understand. Don't question what the Almighty gives you," he chuckled.

One day not too long after, Jacob saw Irene's line nearing the lunch area. He could barely contain himself. He waved to her and after they went through the food line, collecting their bowls of watery turnip soup and tiny pieces of bread, they sat together with Sam. Jacob introduced them. "This is Irene, a very special person in my life."

And so began a passionate relationship. They joined each other whenever their sections broke for lunch at the same time. He began writing her love notes at night in the barracks on scraps of paper.

What a shabby piece of paper, he thought as he looked one over. But the sentiment was real.

"I see a future in your eyes. You will captivate me the rest of my life. We can be so happy together, my princess." Now it sounded corny to him. He read it again. *Well it's the best offer she'll get all day, I'll bet,* he thought, grinning at his own wit.

He presented it to her in the hallway next day. She read it, flashed him a smile, and tucked his heartfelt missive inside her shirt.

"Thank you, Kuba," she said. She liked his nickname.

"I love your intelligence," he told her one evening when they were walking around the camp together.

"You're sweet, Kuba; you're not so bad yourself, you know. I think you're brilliant."

"Wow. Now I have to live up to that. Actually, I want to talk about *you*. You're always fun to be with. And so sexy," he said, taking a long glance at her shapely legs.

"Be careful; don't start something you can't finish," she teased. "You know we have to wait until we get out of here."

"This damn war really cramps a guy's style."

She laughed and there were those butterflies inside him. Yes, this one had possibilities. He hadn't felt like this since Claire.

He put his arm around her; an electric shock went through him. What he wouldn't give for five minutes alone with her. That started him thinking. *I've got to find a way.*

She had come from his home town, Łódź, on an earlier transport by herself. With her soft, flawless skin she was so lovely; he longed to hold her.

He was drawn to so much about her. He loved the way she spoke and how she carried herself. He constantly dreamed about her while he was doing his boring factory work.

The next time they had lunch together he asked "How do they treat you?" hoping they weren't abusing her in some way.

"It's always the same; I wouldn't call it *good*. I wish they would stop staring at me."

"It's because you're so pretty."

"Thank you, but it's probably more like an animal thing, and I don't appreciate it. I wish they'd all drop dead," she whispered.

He laughed. What could they do? The creeps were going to ogle the women one way or the other. As long as they didn't touch her.

"Let me know if they try anything," he said, like he could do anything about it.

"I will," she said as she took her leave. "We've got to go back, Kuba."

He spent the next hour thinking about her. He would charm this sweet dove into his life and keep her. Then no one would ever hurt her again.

They couldn't see each other from their work stations, so he imagined all sorts of scenarios with her and wore a perpetual smile while doing so. He would buy her a house; he would give her diamonds. He would take her around the world.

One day over lunch she said "I'm lucky; I have an easy job so there's less chance of making a mistake."

"Bad news to make a mistake *here,*" Jacob agreed.

"If you get in trouble, it could be the last trouble you'll ever have," she said. "I do get bored, though. It's so mind-numbingly repetitious."

"No kidding. Can you believe we're making *bullets for them to use killing Jews?*"

"I know. Some people sabotage the work, I've heard, but I don't. It's not worth my life."

"You've got *that* right. I'd kind of like you to stay alive, too."

The more time they spent together the closer they got. They were young and love *bloomed.*

Irene managed not to lose much weight. Today she would be termed a 'plus size' girl, still an attractive woman. She also had changes of clothes, like Jacob.

One day on lunch break he asked her where she got the extra food and clothing, keeping his voice low.

"A friend I met here gave them to me," she said quietly, suddenly interested in the graying paint on the wall.

"A boyfriend?" he asked, now on high alert. He didn't need competition here in this awful place. He couldn't even take her to dinner or court her in any kind of style.

She continued to look away.

"It's all right, you can tell me," he prompted, striving mightily for *casual.* "I'm glad you got those things. Really."

Clearly uneasy, she finally said "I have a friend here, Artur, who is a jeweler." That seemed to be all she was going to say.

Jacob wasn't giving up so easily. "How did he get those extra things?"

"Don't tell anyone."

"I won't; I promise," he said, his hand on his heart. *Oh, no.* Now he was breaking out in a sweat. Not a good move; he tried to look relaxed.

"All right," she said. "He smuggled some jewelry in and traded with guards for clothes and food." She glanced around; no one heard.

"A boyfriend?" he asked again, still making a monumental effort to stay cool.

"Not anymore," she said, looking into his eyes. "I have met my man."

Wow. Jacob puffed up like a blowfish, but said nothing. He was so stunned his usual smooth talk deserted him.

She just smiled and squeezed his hand. They had to get back to work.

The rest of the day he worked at double speed. He was a happy man.

"How did your parents meet?" He asked one evening in June while they were walking around camp.

"You won't believe it."

"Well, try me anyway."

"They had an arranged marriage. They had never seen each other before their wedding day."

"Amazing. I thought that was over with in past centuries."

"Leave it to my parents to revive an outdated custom," she chuckled.

"I take it they liked what they saw?"

"Apparently. They've been married over twenty years, and have five children."

"I feel bad when I think about you riding on that train with no family. At least I had Sam."

"It was horrible, Kuba. I leaned up against a wall the whole time. Ugh! Awful, just awful." She shook her head at the floor. "I thought I was going to die."

"I hope you'll never have any more losses. Only good memories from now on. If we had champagne, I'd toast that right now."

She agreed. "Someday."

"My brother Sam volunteered to get on the train with me, otherwise I would have come alone, too. That's why he's here."

"Really? He volunteered? That's unbelievable. Who would do that?" Her eyes were wide with surprise.

"Exactly. Sam is a very special guy."

"I wish I had at least one family member here," she said, with a sad face she didn't often show.

"You can share Sam with me," he joked. "Think of him as your new brother."

She smiled. "Oh, Kuba, that's so sweet. I'd like that."

They rounded the corner of her barracks and sat down to rest near the door.

"Are you closer to your mama or papa?"

"Papa," she said. My mother poured painful medicine on my leg one time and it burned so badly I never forgave her."

"Really? You still can't forgive her?"

"Well, we've never been close like Papa and me. He's so handsome, Mama probably fainted when she saw him at the altar. He's very smart and well-spoken. He has so many friends. I used to watch them while they discussed the plight of the Jews and the war. He was always the leader of the group."

"If he's anything like you, he's a smart cookie."

"Oh, you," she said; she loved it.

One day Jacob and Irene saw the guards beating some prisoners. She quickly looked the other way, her face arranged in stark disapproval. She stared at the ground a few minutes. He knew she was very worried for her family's safety. Jacob let her have some space. She took a few deep breaths and then turned to him with a little smile. He saw she had gathered herself, one of the things he loved about her.

She was strong emotionally; she didn't cry much about her situation. Jacob didn't either, so they didn't often have to shore each other up. That's not to say they didn't come close to breaking at times, with this much physical and mental torture. They did better than most, though.

They had a friend named Thomas, a genius at poetry. He would get up in front of a group of 500 on Sundays and spout wonderful verses, invented on the spot. Jacob could have used some of the poetry for his love letters but he preferred to do his own romancing. He wasn't going to be any Cyrano De Bergerac and have Irene fall in love with *Thomas*.

They were delighted to meet Wilek and his girlfriend Sala, tall, dark-haired intellectuals who loved socializing, even in a prison camp. Each had a great sense of humor. Wilek had his brother Moniek with him. Jacob was glad to know another pair of brothers, although he remained closer to Wilek than he did Moniek.

One Sunday they were sitting around a table, discussing philosophy. "I like Janina Lindenbaum," Irene said.

"Isn't she the one shot by the Nazis?" Wilek asked, pulling his chair up closer to the table.

"I never heard that." Irene blinked at him.

"She studied at the University of Warsaw, my home town. I heard they shot her in 1942." Wilek said.

"Oh my God," Irene's face reddened. She started feeling in her pockets for a tissue.

Jacob saw her pain. He grabbed a piece of cloth nearby and handed it to her, scooting his chair a little closer as he returned to it. "What do you like about her philosophy?" he asked, to distract her.

She warmed to the subject. "She talks about logic, including the *Raven Paradox*. 'If ravens are black and this apple is green, it's not a raven.'" She dabbed at her nose and eyes with the cloth. Jacob watched her carefully, making sure she was alright.

"Why is that a paradox?" asked Wilek's girlfriend, Sala.

"It implies ravens are not green. You can't get information about ravens from apples; maybe some ravens *are* green. You have to find out about ravens from looking at ravens, not apples," Irene replied.

"What's a raven?" asked Sam.

"Similar to a crow," said Moniek.

They all stared at Irene, trying to process this strange philosophy.

"It's a little confusing, but I think I got it," said Sala. "I like Leon Chwistek. He was an odd guy who was also a painter. Do you know his theory of plural realities?" She examined her nails, an old habit, and looked pleased with herself.

"Plural realities – now *there's* a simple topic," cracked Wilek. Sala punched him lightly on the arm.

"I'm getting a headache," complained Ben. "I'm not up to all this. Anybody want to play cards?"

"I like mathematical logic; that sounds like the right philosophy for cards," said Jacob. He put his arm around Irene while Ben dealt the cards. She was fine; she had worked through whatever it was about the philosopher's death. She probably was in a touchy mood today because she missed her family, but it was hard to say. She was complex; Jacob remained utterly fascinated.

Walking back from the card game, Jacob had something to say to Wilek, Moniek, Sala, Ben, Irene and Sam.

He lowered his voice. "I never thought I would hear myself say this, but I've been thinking about cutting a hole in the fence and going out during the night. What do you think?" Jacob said.

"I think you've lost your mind," said Wilek. "Get some rest, Kuba. You'll be yourself tomorrow."

"I know it sounds too dangerous. What do you think, Sam?"

"I don't know. It would be very scary. I don't know if I could do it."

"How about you, Irene?" Jacob looked pleasantly at her, expecting a witty response; however, she was in a serious mood.

"I agree with Wilek. Think about it and you'll realize how hopeless it is. They aren't killing us by the carload here, at least. Maybe we'll live through this to the end of the war."

"Aren't you going to ask *me*?" Ben said.

"I'm almost afraid to," joked Jacob.

"Yes, I seem to remember back in the ghetto you telling me it was suicide to try to sneak out. Remember? A body free of bullet holes?"

"I know, but my imagination runs away with me sometimes. All right, the committee has spoken, and we voted it down," said Jacob. "On to the next item of business."

"The next item is food; do you have any food from your trades with that guy?" Wilek asked. He looked at his brother Moniek. "Jacob is very resourceful and has found a way to get extra food. If you are ever stuck on a desert island, he is the guy to be with."

Jacob laughed. "I don't know about that. Unfortunately, we ate all the food I recently got. Sorry, buddy, I wish I could feed you a steak dinner," said Jacob.

"Don't say things like 'steak dinner'," said Irene. "It's hard to hear it."

"You're right. Let's just take another walk around the grounds," Jacob said, taking her hand. That was everyone's clue to leave them alone.

Jacob finally found an opportunity for quality time with her. One night they snuck off around the back of the barracks. They were sitting nose-to-nose in a dark corner. The guard had moved to a different place for a little bit, very unusual.

"Do you ever get tired of being called names?" she asked.

"You mean like *Dirty Jew?*"

"Yes. I want to punch them in the face."

"Oh," he chuckled. "Don't do *that*. I need you in one piece so I can kiss you enough times, which will be never." He gave her some little kisses to demonstrate.

She laughed. "You're insatiable."

"Only with you," he said, watching out of the corner of his eye for Kapos.

"Do you have trouble sleeping?" he asked.

"Why? Do you?"

"No, as a matter of fact. I fall right asleep. I've always been a good sleeper," he said.

"Sometimes I have problems sleeping. I think I need you there to tuck me in."

For once Jacob blushed. He glanced around to see if anyone heard her.

"I will do that after the war," he said, as they nuzzled. They stayed there for fifteen minutes until the guard returned; how Jacob longed for more of *that* kind of time.

A week later in the evening they were walking around camp together, as they frequently did. It was summer time and the evening brought cool breezes that relieved the day's heat.

"Where are your parents?" he finally asked. He didn't want to cause her pain, but he really wanted to know.

"They wanted me to get out of Łódź when things were getting too dangerous. It was supposed to be safer in a little town nearby where we had some relatives. I was deported from there."

"What about your relatives?"

"They didn't take them with me. I don't know what happened to them or my parents. I keep asking new people that come here, but no one knows anything."

Her family seemed to have just disappeared off the map. Jacob and Sam heard nothing of their family, either, but didn't really expect to. They had been the last of their immediate family.

— ∞∞∞

Since he enjoyed her company so much, he didn't mind Irene's odd traits. He didn't know that before the war, all the boys were afraid of her; she had quite a temper and would verbally attack.

She and Jacob didn't always get along perfectly. She had a sharp mind and could really throw some barbs. He tried to avoid frustrating her; he was too smitten for arguing. He just liked to watch her and listen to her. He learned things from her; about books he hadn't read, and places her grandparents were from.

Jacob had a calming effect on her, just what she needed.

She fought with her friends a lot, though. He thought it was strange, but shrugged it off. They were young and interested in having fun, not analyzing every mood. She continued to think people were against her, and he was too inexperienced to realize Irene was showing symptoms of *Paranoia*.

While she had the symptoms before the war, these circumstances had to have thrown gasoline on that fire. In Hitler's world, everyone really *was* out to get her.

CHAPTER 20

Same Pain, Different Place   7/1944 – 1/1945

*(12) June 5, 1945: A prisoner is liberated by U.S. Army in
Buchenwald and identifies a Nazi guard who
had been brutally beating prisoners. Justice came
a bit late, but it final arrived.*

DOORS AND WINDOWS SHOOK LIKE there were bombs going off ten feet away.
The Allies were getting too close for Nazi comfort, so they chose to move
the factory to another camp, Chestochowa. It was a smaller camp with
5,000 prisoners about 124 miles southwest of Warsaw. Of course prisoners

had to do all the physical labor involved in the transfer. They were weak but still had to place those big machines on rollers and move them out.

Ben, Jacob and Sam walked over to the big machine and helped the others place it on rollers. It was a back-breaking job and afterwards, they stood with their hands on their knees, trying to get their breathing back to normal.

"Push, you Jewish vermin!" The guard glared at them. How dare they stop and rest?

Sam and Ben got on either side of Jacob to push; Jacob mentally cursed the guard. Then he decided not to let the monsters win again. He tried for a jaunty attitude. Maybe if he acted like he was happy and calm, he would actually feel that way.

"Don't stub your toe," he teased Sam. "And Ben, don't you give the officer any dirty looks."

"Would I do that?" He replied.

As they rolled the machine along, it would stall when they came to an uneven piece of ground. They had to stop, count to three and all push as hard as they could to get over the mound of dirt. Jacob, Sam and Ben were on the side of the machine, pulling it along with Ben in front.

Suddenly Ben lost his footing and slipped; he hit the ground, his legs just in front of the machine. At that very moment, the giant rollers lurched forward from the team effort, right over one leg and broke it. The boys who were pushing behind the machine weren't strong enough to get it over the second leg, which they thought was a lump of ground, and it rolled back off of Ben. He grimaced in pain, shrieked and screamed.

Jacob panicked; how could Ben stand up and move normally? He had to fit in. His mind flew through some possibilities. Maybe Ben could lean on him, pretend to be pushing.

"*Get up, Ben!*" he urged. "*Don't Scream! Get up!*"

Ben was in far too much pain to stay quiet and his involuntary cries were shrill and constant. The SS officer glanced his way. The spawn of hell in the black cap and uniform sauntered over with his hand resting on his pistol, and took a look at him.

"Get up, Ben!" Jacob urged him again, knowing Ben had only a few seconds left to save himself.

Moaning, Ben tried to move his leg but was totally unable. He cried "Oh, God help me, help me."

The SS man lifted his gun and took aim. Poor Ben turned his head away and squeezed his eyes shut. It took everything Jacob had not to attack that officer. He balled his fists so tightly his fingernails dug into the palms of his hands.

Bang! Shot in the head, Ben crumpled instantly. The horrid noise felt like a blow square on Jacob's forehead; staggering backwards, he almost passed out himself. Then he instinctively moved forward and searched Ben's body for signs of life. There weren't any. The damage to his head was too great.

"You! Get back to work!" The guard yelled, glaring at him. The guard rolled Ben's body out of the way, kicking and shoving it with his foot.

You piece of human garbage, thought Jacob, as he put on his best worker-face. He didn't want to die, too. Sam was gasping for air next to him, on the verge of a full-blown panic attack. Jacob swallowed an enormous amount of shock and fury and got back in line quickly. He turned to Sam and spoke sharply.

"Get yourself together unless you want to die, too."

Sam somehow got into control again. Swallowing down the fear and anguish, Jacob and Sam continued pulling the machine along.

"Good, Sam. Just keep putting one foot in front of the other. You have to be an actor to stay alive."

Sam nodded his head, but said nothing. He appeared to be in some kind of trance, but thank God he kept working. Jacob tried to still his shaking hands by gripping the machine harder. He hoped Sam wouldn't be terribly damaged by all this, so he could have a happy life after the Allies won the war.

He looked back only once at Ben; just a few minutes earlier he had been chatting with him. Seeing Ben's lifeless form caked in blood and dirt made Jacob gag from the rage. It was like he had just bitten into something bitter and poisonous. Warm saliva filled his mouth.

Oh, no. Don't throw up. He swallowed again and again. If he started retching, he might be shot. *Please help me, God.* He managed to get past it and keep on working.

Briefly he wondered, *What good is life anyway? Is it worth all this pain?* But he didn't toy with that for long; it was the *wrong* road to go down.

In spite of his efforts, that much rage was hard to keep stuffed down. As he pushed the machine and felt his muscles strain and tremble, he found some relief in fantasies of revenge; it was part of his daily routine. They all had their favorite scenarios of how they would torture and kill Nazis.

Then he reminded himself: the SS were an elite force of murderers. They weren't going to waste time mending a Jewish prisoner's leg. He needed to toughen up and remember: prisoners were just objects. Broken things go in the trash; simple as that. *Don't expect anything but misery and torture from the SS and you won't be disappointed.*

Once they got to the camp, they collapsed on their new bunks. Jacob's head was spinning with anger, fear, and desire for revenge. He realized Ben would not be getting a new bunk. He felt utterly hollow inside.

He was restless. They were so dirty and sweaty. "Let's get rid of a couple layers of dirt and clothes. We can wash them tomorrow," he suggested.

As they did so, he had to continually quell his emotions for his own sake, as well as Sam's. He stepped into the shower and took a minute to be grateful it didn't happen to Sam and him. Still, the tears flowed for his dear companion.

He hoped he would find Irene soon, and worried and searched until he saw her in the food line the next day. He waved joyfully at her and she waved back. Thank God.

Death, formerly a passenger on the train, had departed the cattle car with them and now shadowed them wherever they went, a malevolent spirit.

Sometimes he could chase away the evil presence hovering around him for a little while. But at night, when he crawled onto his mattress bag, it was lying there, grinning at him. Or so it felt. *Tomorrow could be your last day.*

He became skilled at kicking that guy off the mattress. He was *not* going to give in to gloom and doom. He would say his prayers, send out his love to his family, think about Irene, and be off to sleep.

While alive, Mama never knew how much her love would help them through this, but her spirit was there now and she surely could see them struggle. Jacob believes she sent them strength. She lives on today in spirit and he frequently feels her presence.

The Germans were retreating on all fronts, blowing up railroad tracks that would steer the Allies toward the camps. If the prisoners had known that, it might have crushed the frail little strands of hope for rescue they were nurturing. How would the Allies find them?

The world was still upside down. Good people were in prison. The real criminals were free to do as they liked, and they did. Many lived a life of luxury. *Police* were murdering people. It was a capital crime to have a radio. Nothing made sense any more.

Fortunately the world was going to right itself soon.

Back at work in the factory, they listened to the booming sound of artillery as it got closer and louder each day. Jacob, Sam and Irene were now experiencing joy for the first time in a very long time; when the windows rattled or the ceiling shook, Jacob had to suppress a little smile. The guards were getting more and more nervous. Their eyes darted around and settled on them with malicious intent. Prisoners had to be extremely careful to hide their smiles and not let Nazis even suspect their elation.

In January of 1945 they had been living surrounded by guards, guns and fences in one place or another a long, weary five years. At midnight, January 15th-16th, the Nazis vanished. The guard towers were empty.

CHAPTER 21

Sweet Freedom   JAN. / 1945 - FEB. / 1945

Jacob, age 23 - Walbrzych, Poland;
town where he and Irene married
(Dr. Eisenbach's collection)

SAM AND JACOB WERE AWAKENED in the night by wild shouting and cheering. Worn down as his body was, the excitement infused Jacob with fresh energy. He leaped from his straw palette and ran to the barracks door with

Sam right behind him. Prisoners outside were shouting "We're free! The war's over!" For such broken-down people, unusually strong voices rose up in triumph.

"Come look! The guard towers are empty!" one yelled in their direction. The poor man was so thin, Jacob wondered if he would survive the walk through the gate. He said a little prayer for him and the others like him. Especially the few children in camp.

Still, was this another fantasy? Was the man brain-damaged from starvation? Jacob was cautious. This had to be a mistake; guards just didn't desert their posts. Not in Hitler's army.

For so long they lived one day at a time and tried not to think about freedom. Still, colorful images of home and joyous reunions with family regularly cropped up in radiant color to torment them like some mirage in the desert.

The thought of being rescued was something Jacob didn't entertain too often. If he tortured himself with it he might crack, so he kept the focus on *today*. When the Nazis actually *left*, it took a while for that to sink in.

Sam and he silently padded over to the hated towers and gazed upward. There they stood: empty, ghosts looming up out of the dark to engulf them.

They backed away from the towers, fearful that a guard's face would suddenly appear up there in the darkened window.

They walked through the camp looking for Irene, calling her name. Her bed was empty. Finally they found her; she was wandering around with a small group of women. She ran toward him into his open arms.

"What do you think?" she asked, her voice shrill. "Oh, Kuba, I heard they ambush people. When we go out the gate, they'll shoot us."

Jacob held her, trembling, in his arms while his mind raced away. *Is this too good to be true? Is this a trap?* Jacob wondered, his heart sinking. He didn't know what to think.

But -- he was the man; he would figure it out. "Come on, Sweetheart. Let's ask around," he said as he took her hand. Irene wasn't any softie most of the time, and he relished this chance to take care of her.

They walked with Sam through camp, carefully checking things out. They asked other prisoners if they had seen any guards lurking around, and no one had. No matter where they looked, there were no guards. Good God! It seemed they actually *WERE* free. They heard joyous shouts but this time the excited words were their own.

The guards had been ordered to *run for their lives* immediately. They didn't take time to shoot prisoners. If they'd had an hour's notice, Jacob wouldn't be alive today. They fled, leaving everything behind. God was finally intervening on a grand scale.

The Jewish camp leader, whom Jacob calls 'a great man', cautioned them "Don't leave yet. Wait until morning; there is gunfire all over out there."

They looked at each other and swallowed hard. They might have to run a gauntlet of bullets. Beads of perspiration appeared on Jacob's suddenly-warm face.

The leader continued, "Remember *don't* overeat when you find food; you'll get sick. We're not out of danger by any means. Germany has not surrendered yet. If they capture you, they'll kill you. Plus, there are still plenty of anti-Semites around with their crowbars. Watch yourself."

They were sufficiently scared by that to think rationally. While others raced willy-nilly out of camp to whatever fate awaited them, Sam, Irene and Jacob followed directions. When it was daylight, they walked through the gate together, fully alive and bursting with joy. The sun was bright and the day was clear and cold. Jacob took a moment to honor Ben's memory; how he would have enjoyed this. Then angry hunger pangs reminded him of their first priority. They had to find some kind of food.

Luck smiled on them once again. Better than that; they won the lottery. They came across a well-stocked German truck. They stared at the bread, cheese, sausage, even vodka. Jacob wanted to dive in there in the middle of it. They grabbed as much as they could carry and took it with them. They had to use restraint and make it last; their stomachs couldn't handle too much food. But it was *there:* for eating now, or for them to take along and have later. It was *their* choice. How precious that new freedom was.

That night they stayed in a five-star hotel: the Nazi barracks. Crisp sheets, tasty food, vodka – they were in heaven. What delightful revenge, for bedraggled survivors to live in their captor's quarters, eat their food, drink their vodka, and sleep on their sheets. God was good.

"Remember, Sam? I said we would have a party when we were free?"

"You sure did," said Sam, who tasted the vodka and made a face. "How do people enjoy this stuff?"

"I think you get used to it. How about you, Sweetheart? Do you like it?"

"It's okay," said Irene. "We can bring it along on our trip home to keep us warm."

They were 100 miles from Łódź. They were desperate to know who was still alive in their families, but there was no way to find out right away. They had to go home and wait to see who came back. Finding loved ones became the number-one mission, but first they had to find a means to get home. They would get a good night's sleep and start off in the morning.

Their friends Wilek Pachter and girlfriend Sala lived in Warsaw, so in the morning they parted but would keep in touch. Sam, Irene and Jacob started walking.

They only got three miles before they had to turn around. Sam was still wearing wooden shoes, developed terrible blisters and couldn't walk. They were all desperate to get out of there and Sam was concerned he was holding them back.

Jacob looked at his worried face. "Sam, you're my brother and nothing you need is too much trouble. Besides, you volunteered to come to camp with me. You helped keep me alive. Don't you worry; we'll find a way." He put his arm around Sam's slender shoulders. He was weak and appeared to be emotionally exhausted. Jacob knew the feeling all too well.

Sam nodded gratefully and hobbled along with them. Irene also re-assured her new brother there was nothing to worry about. They were free; that was all that mattered.

On their way back to the Nazi barracks, they struggled along sup-porting Sam. A Russian soldier came by in a truck.

"Good morning. Do you need a ride?"

They shrank back; Russians had been Hitler's allies, after all. And they were *armed*.

"I think we..." Jacob hesitated.

"Don't worry, I won't bite" he smiled. "Trust me, we all hate Adolf Hitler now; we're on your side."

They looked doubtful.

"We won't hurt you. Come on, hop in."

"Let's go," urged Irene. "Sam can't walk anymore; if he tries to walk any distance, he might damage his feet."

The Russian seemed sincere, so they decided to trust him, and climbed into his truck.

Those wonderful souls were very kind to them. If they were hungry, the Russians brought them to the front of the food line because when the line was long, sometimes the food ran out. Russians were *brutal* to the German people, but kind to those who were Hitler's victims. They even gave them tubes of powder to get rid of lice, which they were thrilled to have. That one small kindness after they'd been so cruelly treated almost made Jacob cry.

Somebody cares that we have lice.

To get home they had to take a train, and they had to wait a month for them to be operational. Meanwhile they tried to enjoy their freedom and plan for the future, now that they had one.

They stayed with the Russian soldiers in the buildings they were occupying. There were empty dwellings around where people had fled, leaving their things behind. Many people were terrified of the Russians; you never knew what to expect during that time of insanity, but the Russians were not harming Polish people, at least from what they saw. Jacob looked at the vacant places and thought sadly of his home. Was it an empty shell, or were there people in it? Did any of his family come back to it? He could hardly wait to get home and find out.

Survival was by no means guaranteed; there was a widespread shortage of food. People were all helping each other. One thought kept them going. They would get home and find their loved ones.

They never imagined reality was going to deliver such a knockout blow.

—∞∞∞—

Finally the trains were running. With no tickets, and the train full anyway, they climbed up a railroad car and sat on the roof. They tied themselves to the iron bars with their belts.

The brisk ride was freezing, but they were so ecstatic to be alive the cold was somehow bearable; they all had on numerous layers of clothing. Jacob held Irene's hand. The three of them laughed at their silly jokes, sang their favorite songs and planned for their future; Jacob would go to dental school. Irene and he mused about the children they would have.

"I have a joke," said Sam.

"Tell us," Irene said with a big smile.

"What looks like a human being, walks around and talks, but has nothing inside?"

"A robot?" asked Jacob. Sam shook his head, grinning.

"A ghost?" said Irene.

"No; a Nazi!"

Jacob stared at him. *He's worse off than I thought; maybe he's in shock.*

"You need to change your taste in humor, buddy. There's nothing funny about those murdering fiends. You should know that."

"Why are you giving me a bad time?" grumbled Sam.

"I'm sorry. You know I don't mean to. I'm just surprised and a little worried that you are in shock or something."

"I'm not in shock. I just wanted to laugh at them."

Laugh at them? Jacob and Irene rolled their eyes at each other. Either Sam was in denial, or he was a lot farther along in recovery than they were; they found *nothing* humorous about those monsters. They did know recovery was going to take time, for all of them.

Sam sat up straight and announced: "I am going to join the Polish army. I'm a true patriot and I'm going to serve my country. Do you think it's too late? Could I do that?"

"Sure. It's a good idea but only if you can stay safe. There are still a lot of Jew-haters around, and traditionally the army hasn't treated Jews so well," Jacob cautioned.

Sam sounded somewhat naïve considering what they'd suffered, but that was his nature. He was a trusting soul. He shrugged. "I'll just change my name to something that doesn't sound Jewish."

Jacob hoped that would do the trick. "You let us know if you are mistreated. Irene and I will stay in Łódź unless we find too much prejudice there."

They enjoyed their train-top adventure all the way home, lice free. The loud clackety-clack of wheels on the rails was teeth-rattling but fun, except on the turns; those were hair-raising. The sort of excitement they'd gladly pay for at an amusement park, but here, they would rather not have that particular thrill. There was no safety net. One old, worn-out belt breaking, one careless slip and fall off the train would kill them. Jacob thinks the train officials knew they were there, but looked the other way; he doesn't know if they worried about their safety.

At that point, people still weren't fully informed about the camps. The conductor might have thought they were just drifters. If he had known what they'd suffered, maybe he would have brought them into a passenger car and let them sit on the floor, at least. It would be a while before the news spread about the extent of the depravity and the millions of victims.

It was stop-and-go traveling. It took a full day to go that 100-mile distance but to them, it was traveling in great style, because they weren't on foot or in a cattle car.

When they could see Łódź ahead, they shrieked for joy. At last! They would finally reunite with their families.

More horror awaited them.

CHAPTER 22

Life After Living Death --- Healing   1945

(13) Lwów Ghetto, Spring 1942, where his sister was with her new husband. They were probably both killed in a street massacre there.

HOME! THE SIGHT OF ŁÓDŹ was indescribable. Never mind the war damage, the widespread looting that had been done, and that ugly ghetto; everyone would pitch in and bring their city back to its former glory. They found an empty apartment and moved in. Their total net worth amounted to their few pieces of clothing and their tubes of lice powder.

They foraged around like hungry mice for what they could find. Then a Jewish organization began delivering food to them.

They registered with the office that was set up to reunite families. Survivors trickled in, but not one person from Jacob's or Irene's family had returned. Still, they remained hopeful. It took a person a while to get back from wherever the Nazis had them.

He looked for their neighbor Ruben's name, but didn't find it anywhere. He learned their cousin Marysia, the pharmacist, went to Argentina in 1938. He couldn't find any trace of cousin Fela, Aunt Anne, Aunt Esther, cousin Schmul and his family, any of Ben's family who might not know about his death, or Jacob's ex-girlfriend Claire and her family. Friend David and his family were nowhere to be found, either. Not finding them wasn't necessarily a bad thing; they might still be alive. Cousin Lolek wasn't accounted for. He hoped he had somehow survived. Irene was trying to find siblings and her parents but there was no word of them. Sadly, there was no sign of Henry or Papa, either.

He did find news of his sister. At the registration place he met a woman who had gone to Lwów like Fela did. He asked her about it.

"Your sister was Fela Eisenbach? I knew her."

"Yes," Jacob said. "One day she just stopped writing us. She was only 18. Do you know what happened to her?"

"Yes, I think I do. She met a man and they married. He was a nice young fellow; such a sweet couple. Then I fled with the Russians when the Nazis attacked the red army. I ended up in Siberia, which was like a frozen nightmare, but I managed to survive."

"That's wonderful," he said, holding her hands in his.

She was probably sixty-five or seventy years old, had a scarf tied around her head for warmth and fingers starting to twist with rheumatism. He could only imagine the pain that went untreated in the cold of Siberia, and was amazed she survived that grueling trek to Russia.

She rubbed her forehead and sighed. "If your sister went with the Russians, she would probably have been able to contact you at some point."

She massaged her fingers over and over. "My hands got so much worse in the cold." She looked down like she didn't want to go on. Jacob urged her to tell him more about Fela, bracing himself.

She looked steadily at him with such sadness in her eyes. "I'm so sorry, but your sister and her husband were probably killed in one of two mass shootings done in Lwów in 1941 and 1943. Nazis came through with machine guns, and assisted by Ukrainians, spent three days gunning down 110,000 Jews, then in 1943 they liquidated the rest of the Jews in the Lwów ghetto."

That staggered him, though he tried not to show much reaction and make her feel guilty for telling him.

He remembered a picture of Fela holding a little dog. In spite of his attempts to be strong, he started to choke up when an image of the massacres came to him: his sister bloody and crumpled on the street, perhaps her new husband curled up next to her. Jacob had seen way too much senseless horror.

The kindly woman was studying his face. With tremendous effort, he pushed his hurt aside. "It's all right," he said with one deep breath. "It's certainly not *your* fault. I'm grateful for the news."

They hugged, wished each other God speed and moved on.

As they parted, he silently cursed Hitler once again and let his tears flow. He'd have liked to dig up Hitler and kill him again.

His beautiful, intelligent sister was never heard from again. There would be no nieces and nephews from her.

The next time he saw the old woman, he still felt bad for her. He had the presence of mind this time to ask about her and her family. She had found a couple people, though not nearly enough. They chatted a little and moved on. After that, he remembered her in his prayers.

They discovered their childhood home was occupied. Jacob stared at it for a long while.

"What's wrong, Honey?" Irene was right there to soothe him.

"Where are they? Is *everybody* gone?" Jacob stopped a minute to control his outrage. "Papa, Fela and Henry; all our cousins, aunts and uncles. How can they *all* be dead if we are alive? Why are we so lucky and no one else is?"

"It will be okay, Kuba. We'll find some of them," Sam quietly commented, though he, too, looked to be suffering.

"You didn't expect them to be *here*, did you?" Irene asked. "Surely this home was taken when you moved out of it to the ghetto."

He didn't answer, because suddenly he was pulled back through time. He could smell Mama's delicious cooking; hear the joy in the chattering of his aunts and uncles. The front door opened and closed repeatedly as relatives and friends bustled in and brought laughter and gifts. He enjoyed the warmth of the kitchen and of Mama's hugs once more. There was Papa, showing them a new bedspread being made at the factory. Fela was in the corner talking on the telephone, relaxing in an easy chair. Sam and Henry were playing ball with the cousins. It was like a warm bath. Peaceful and cozy.

"Remember, Sam? How it used to be when we were all together? The cousins came to visit, we laughed and played ball? Those wonderful meals Mama served?"

The stricken look on Sam's face snapped Jacob back to the present. He didn't need to add to everyone's pain. That was over and done with now.

"I didn't mean to upset you, Sam, I'm sorry." He stopped to take a few breaths. "We'll make our own secure future. You, me and Irene. And you'll find a wife and we'll all have children. A new start, Sam. It will be good."

Sam nodded in agreement. "Sounds like a play," he said.

"What?"

"*You, Me and Irene.* Maybe I'll write all this down someday. I mean, when I'm out of the army." He smiled a little.

It delighted Jacob to hear Sam talk of future plans; he breathed a sigh of relief.

He looked over at the apartment again. Jacob didn't cry easily, but he *was* full of rage. He had to turn away from it; he wouldn't stand there and look at it anymore.

He felt Irene at his side, nudging him, putting her arm around him. "It will turn out okay," she said, no doubt trying to convince herself, too.

His pain about this was stubborn; his deepest roots were in this place. "Strangers are living in my *home*, Irene."

"I know; mine too. But we have to move on and rebuild our lives. There's no other direction to go." She gazed at him, a challenge in her eyes. She knew he was made of the right stuff to overcome this and have a productive life.

"We can do it together, Kuba," put in Sam. "I know we can." Sweet Sam; always there for him.

Fueled by the love of this new little family as well as loving family members who had passed away, he was able to step away from that precipice which threatened to swallow him if he gave in to the anger and hate.

"You know what? We CAN!" he said, taking in the looting and bomb damage and all the devastation around him. "We are better than this. We're not going to let this defeat us. We have beaten Hitler; we can do anything we put our minds to."

Irene and Sam had big smiles. "That's the Jacob we know!" said Irene. He was a winner, a natural leader, and she was proud of him. They gave him the strength he needed right then, but many times he was able to help them, and that made his chest expand with joy and his heartbreak mend a little more.

They tried to get on with life. There were no stores where people could buy food or clothing. Communists were taking control; it was illegal to own a business. Farmers were fearful to let go of their crops. It was an odd time. They lived in a kind of frontier; a society without order. People just found empty places to live and moved in; they didn't have to pay rent.

Week after week, for months and months they checked on family; no one signed in. Not even anyone in the 100-person extended family.

One day he got some very distressing information. He hurried home where Sam and Irene were doing some cleaning. He burst in the door in a rage.

"What, Kuba?" Sam asked, holding a cleaning rag and bottle of soapy liquid.

"Papa is probably dead, Sam."

Sam's expression changed completely; he dropped the materials and ran to Jacob. "How do you know that?"

Irene came in the room. Her newly-washed hair was in pin curls wrapped in a scarf. "What did you find out?"

"I met a man at the Committee Center who had been in Papa's group of 600 men they deported. At the camp they starved these men; made them do useless work like carrying heavy stones from one place to another, in twenty below zero weather, and ... " Jacob went silent, unable to say the words.

"It's okay, Honey," Irene said. "Tell us."

Jacob drew in a shaky breath. "He was weak, you know, and just skin and bones. He didn't last too long doing that. He's just a pile of ashes now." He sat down on the sofa and put his face in his hands. Irene looked from one to the other, and remained quiet.

"He was a good Papa," said Sam, tears streaming down his face. "How could they? Those murdering fiends!" He joined Jacob on the couch. "I can't stand it anymore. Everyone's gone."

Jacob heard the call to action down deep, the one he always responded to. He shook off his momentary collapse and looked at Sam. "We can stand it because we have to. Mama is here and probably Papa, too. He's thinking '*Why aren't you getting that cleaning done? Don't cry over me. I'm doing great here with Mama and a lot of others.*'"

"Do you really think he and Mama are together?"

"I absolutely know it, Sam. Without a doubt. So we can be happy for them because they are dancing on a cloud together, or singing in a choir, or maybe flying around sightseeing. Imagine being able to fly anywhere you wanted."

Sam looked thoughtful. "I guess you're right. But I still miss them terribly."

"Me, too" said Jacob. "When we die, a *long* time from now, we'll see them then and maybe even fly around with them."

They laughed at that idea. The three went into the kitchen to fix some lunch. Jacob prayed for continued strength to help his little family recover.

Sometimes when he stopped struggling for survival, the anger and pain cropped up and overwhelmed him like some greedy highway robber waiting in the shadows. It was easy to shut down. He had to stay busy and productive to outrun the pain. That way he could absorb it a little at a time, at his own pace. There were so many losses to grieve, it was staggering.

One afternoon when the pain was clawing away at his peace of mind, he took a walk to think things over.

What a crime against everything sacred and cherished to have millions of people die for one man's glorification. Perhaps Hitler's selfish ego gratification is the worst part of it all. If our family died fighting in a war, at least we would have their patriotism to think about. But they were simply slaughtered to glorify this evil, greedy demon.

There's nothing of the family to save and remember, like army medals. There isn't even a grave to put flowers on. They were thrown in ditches or burned.

Here he stopped to shed some tears, then breathed deep and continued walking.

Poor Henry went ignominiously to his death in the back of a truck in a pile of sick people. I so hope their ends were quick and not agonizing. I know what Nazis are capable of. Please, God, don't let them have been tortured.

Jacob didn't survive everything to come home and waste away from depression and anger, though. He had a choice: be utterly miserable or accept things and be happy, or at least content and optimistic. He chose option two, and would do so for the rest of his life.

There was a lot to do. Day-to-day life was difficult. There were no medical clinics. Sam, Irene, Jacob and some other friends, eight in total, lived together in an empty two-bedroom apartment. The government owned all property and they weren't charging anything at the moment. No one had money anyway.

The price of clothing remained out of reach. Jacob had one pair of pants which Irene ruined by ironing and burning a large hole in the front. They laughed about it. He doesn't remember what he wore in the following weeks; obviously he found *something*, he says, because he wasn't arrested for parading around town without pants.

The majority of people in Łódź were now non-Jewish. Most of them were kind, but some were anti-Semitic and treated them coldly, blaming them for the war; the ultimate irony.

If anyone was ever totally blameless in a war, it was the Jews in this one, Jacob thought bitterly.

CHAPTER 23

Wedding Bells 1945-1946

Dr. Eisenbach, age 30
(Dr. Eisenbach's collection)

LIFE MOVED ON. JACOB LOCATED his friend Srul who had dodged a terrible fate in the selection committee process by sneaking out of his group into Jacob's. They socialized after the war.

Jacob found a small job in Walbrzych, a town in Southwest Poland that's known for its beautiful medieval castle. They moved there, joined by Wilek and Sala, their friends from the camp, who found nothing to come home to in Warsaw. They began to sell things for some extra money. They bought and resold coffee, cigarettes, and little things like that.

A group of Jewish businessmen brought in truckloads of goods for them to sell.

Sam stayed behind in Łódź, pursuing his military career. He sent them postcards sometimes with army news. Jacob was thrilled that Sam was enjoying life.

Wilek and Sala came over one day with news.

"Greetings, my friend," Wilek said, hugging Jacob. "Guess what? Sala and I are getting married on December 20 here in Walbrzych. We want you there as our honored guests."

"Congratulations," Jacob said, shaking his hand. "Let me tell Irene." He called her to come in the room; she was thrilled with the news.

"I have a surprise for you, too, Wilek" he said, feeling like a sly fox. "We will join you and make it a double wedding."

Wilek whooped in delight and hugged Sala. This was news to Irene, too; her eyes lit up like Roman candles. They were all so excited, maybe too much so for poor people; now they had to pay for a wedding.

Nevertheless they planned the wedding and had a beautiful double ceremony in the local Synagogue on December 20, 1945.

The ladies walked up the aisle toward the grooms looking radiant. They carried flowers and looked more beautiful than ever to their men. They joined the grooms under the *chupah* and the Rabbi performed the ceremony.

Wilek and Jacob each served as best man for the other, and the ladies did the same as maids of honor; they giggled over signing their new last names on the certificates.

Their reception featured a lovely wedding cake and all the trimmings.

"A double wedding where all four survived the same Nazi camp; it must be one for the record books," said Wilek.

"Now if only we could afford a honeymoon," said Jacob.

"Really," said Irene, "it's okay; we'll live on love, right, Kuba?"

"Absolutely."

They were still struggling for economic survival, but being newlyweds was exciting and energizing. They had a life to build, children to have, and Jacob's career in dentistry to develop.

Jacob wrote Sam about the wedding. "We hope to see you soon. I think by that time you'll have attracted a lovely young lady into your life. You have accomplished much and you won't have any trouble with that. I hope you are not being bothered by any Jew-haters there. Remember to keep a low profile. We'll celebrate when you get here, all our good fortune so far."

When he heard of Hitler's suicide, Jacob was smug, like everyone else. But then he felt cheated. Adolf was not made to account for himself. How satisfying it would have been to hear him try to justify his reign of terror, or to see him remain mute when questioned, facing his own death. He wouldn't have needed to talk; just sit there in chains. That would have been enough.

Eventually Jacob discovered three cousins living in Germany whom he visited years later. He was grateful to have them; they grew up together in his home town and were very close.

Irene, too, lost all her people except a younger brother. They didn't find out about him right away because he was living in Italy. Later he moved to Israel and they visited him there.

Jacob, Sam and Irene kept in touch with the Jewish Committee and continued to check on the location of family and friends. Time after time, they were crushed with fresh disappointment. Once again, Jacob paced back and forth, asking himself, *How could this be? Everybody??*

Well, there were those cousins in Australia and Marysia, the pharmacist. *But still, everybody else in our whole extended family??*

Each time he would surmount that grief and find a way to be productive.

There were still Jew-haters around after the war. In April 1946 Polish anti-Semites kidnapped a 10-year-old Polish boy. They said Jews killed him and used his blood for making *matzo* (flat bread). A ridiculous story, just to fan the flames of hate.

In the city of Kielce, Poland where a few thousand Jews lived, the anti-Semites went crazy over the story about the kidnapped boy and killed 43 innocent Jews who survived the Holocaust. As a result of the *Kielce Pogrom*, 100,000 Jews left east Europe within three months. Irene and Jacob were two of them.

CHAPTER 24

Cloak And Dagger Time   1947

(14) Bombing by the Luftwaffe, Seige of Warsaw 1939

HE HAD EXPERIENCED ENOUGH VIOLENCE for ten lifetimes. Jacob and Irene escaped Poland through the Jewish organization *Bricha,* which was based in Palestine.

Cloak-and-dagger style, they were smuggled out in the middle of the night. Jacob's heart pounded like a kettle drum as they hurried along. He was tortured by memories of death on the side of the road when the Nazis first came. Would the communists come after them with airplane fire?

They didn't, but it took several hours on the cold, dark path to get into Czechoslovakia. His backpack was heavy and he stumbled and fell; it gave him a few seconds to rest, but the *Bricha* people kept rushing them.

"Keep going! Don't stop!"

Finally they got there, weak with relief. The Czechs welcomed them warmly and gave them hot, delicious meals. Jacob didn't realize how hungry he was until he smelled that food. The bread and butter alone was worth the trip. It was so good to eat heartily in a safe place. He'd almost forgotten the feeling.

Afterwards they directed Jacob and Irene to move on for their own protection. They rode in a comfortable, well-kept train to Prague where they stayed a few days. It was like a honeymoon. Then they went to the American side of Germany.

It didn't bother him that he was in the country that had spawned Hitler's Nazi party; that was all over with, and Jacob was here for his dream: to finish his education in dentistry at the University of Frankfurt. He knew German well enough to take courses in that language without a problem. Also, there were many Americans there. They settled in and before long, there was some exciting news.

Jacob was going to be a father.

CHAPTER 25

The Ghost Of Hitler   1947-1949

Colonel Sam in the Polish army
(Dr. Eisenbach's collection)

AT THE AGE OF ONLY 22 Sam fulfilled his dream and became a colonel in the Polish army, one rank under a general. He was brilliant; in charge of 10,000 soldiers at such a young age. The army stationed him at Bialystock.

A darkness hung over that city; it was very anti-Semitic. Before he went there he changed his name to Stanislaw Adamowski, forced once again to hide his heredity. He was still optimistic that things would be fine.

He wrote them, describing life in the army and his duties. He was thrilled to have been promoted to colonel. He had such loyalty to his country, and believed he was doing a good thing. He congratulated Jacob and Irene on their wedding and said they would get together soon and celebrate it.

They were happy to hear it, but were concerned for his safety. With good reason, it turned out.

One day in 1947, Jacob came home to a letter from cousin Lolek, the one who came to dinner the night Schmul was there. He was living in Łódź. He was excited to see who had written him. Some good news at last! There was still no word from anyone else in the family.´

As he read, though, his joy turned into anguish, as black as the bottom of the sea.

Dear Cousin,

I am so sorry to bring you this terrible news. Sam has been murdered by anti-Semites in his home.

Here is what I have learned. Sam came home from work and put his keys on the table, took off his coat and hung up his hat. Then he walked to the bedroom. Perhaps he heard something in there.

He stood in the doorway. Someone was waiting there, an angry, anti-Semitic person. We don't know if Sam saw the assassin, talked to him, or if he realized what was happening. We do know the intruder shot Sam in the head. There was no evidence of a struggle.

He collapsed at his bedroom door and the end finally came for your precious brother. May he rest in peace in God's love and care.

It sickens me beyond endurance; I can still hardly believe it. Sam survived the war only to be murdered by a Hitler fanatic. It's like the ghost of Hitler came and snatched him back into his clutches.

I have contacted the police in Bialystock and demanded an investiga-
tion. They are not interested in pursuing it. What is wrong with people?
Will this never end?

Sam was buried in Bialystock with military honors; you can visit his
grave if you wish. I went there and it is at a beautiful site.

I can't believe there is still such hate for Jews in our own country.
Next time you are in Łódź, please come visit. We can rebuild our lives
together. I have plans for a good future. I'd like to hear your plans.

God bless you,
Lolek

"Irene!" Jacob cried out in anguish. He crumpled up on the couch and
sobbed.

She ran to his side and read the letter.

"Oh my God, Kuba, I can't believe it. This can't be true! Oh, my
poor sweetheart." She held him as he poured out his pain in a flood of
tears.

He remained depressed for a time and then anger took over.

He was furious that he wasn't able to help Sam in his hour of need.
Of course, it wasn't his fault, but he still wished mightily that he had
been able to be there for his sweet, loyal brother.

He complained bitterly that he had been unable to save either of his
brothers. Irene reminded him, "How is one boy supposed to stop Hitler?
Whole countries failed at it." He knew she was right but he still wished
he could go back in time and help Sam and Henry.

Whenever he thought of this, he had to stop himself and turn to
work. Staying busy helped, but the anger didn't leave.

He would not visit the grave; he resolved to never set foot in that city.
In fact, now he wanted to leave Europe entirely.

Since he was in dental school, he escaped the pain with his studies.
The harder he worked, the better he felt, but the loss of Sam was crush-
ing. They had an incredible bond which has lasted all these years after
Sam's death.

They decided to leave Europe permanently. Too much violence and too many wars. Things were happening fast. Truman signed the 1948 Displaced Persons Act that allowed 200,000 Jews to come to the U.S. That was their ticket. To live in one of the greatest countries ever would fulfill his childhood dream.

They planned to leave for the United States as soon as he graduated from dental school.

Meanwhile, Irene had a healthy pregnancy and Jacob was thrilled, if a little nervous.

Finally the day came. At the hospital, he paced around the waiting room, a typical new father. He tried to read magazines, or study a little. After a long wait, the nurse came out and announced he had a son, heathy and robust. Jacob wanted to race down the hall shouting the news.

They named him Harry and were absolutely delighted with him, until they experienced a few screaming newborn fits at 2:00 a.m. But they adjusted, like all new parents do, and *Baby Makes Three* could have been their song.

Now it was time to finish dental school and get out of there. He was done with Europe.

CHAPTER 26
Sailing The Titanic Route   1950

*(15) U.S.S. General S.D. Sturgis (Ap-137) at Yokohama in
September 1945; in the foreground are dignitaries she carried
to Japan for the Japanese surrender ceremony.*

FOLLOWING GRADUATION IN DENTISTRY IN 1950, toddler Harry and his delighted parents left Frankfurt and came to the U.S. aboard the *S.S. General
Sturgis,* the ship that had taken dignitaries to Yokohama in September,
1945 for the Japanese surrender ceremony.

They sailed in October across the North Atlantic – Titanic territory.
Storms raged the entire ten days, but fortunately they had no mishaps

with icebergs. The ship went up 30 to 40 feet and back down again. It was the wildest roller coaster one could imagine; Jacob relished the trip and had no seasickness. Irene, on the other hand, was green the whole time.

"Papa" he heard from below while he was standing on deck. He looked down to see Harry smiling at him with the wind blowing his hair. He was doing fine at sea. Irene dropped him off and tottered back to bed. Harry reached up for Jacob to pick him up and Jacob held him as they went up and down, again and again in the salty air. The boy's little cheeks were all ruddy and his eyes shone with delight.

Jacob studied his cherubic features and a voice from the past came to mind. *Where you go, I go.* He studied the sea and let thoughts of Sam surround him. His wide, trusting eyes and his patriotic belief in his country. His naiveté in signing up for the army and being willing to go to a Jew-hating city. That just by changing his name, he would be protected. He breathed a sigh of regret. *If only he had listened to me.*

He looked at Harry and suddenly realized *My little boy is living out Sam's words.*

Where you go, I go.

His heart swelled with mixed emotions. Grief for the loss of Sam, but what joy to hold this little angel in his arms.

Jacob, you're so dramatic, you should be in the movies, he told himself, chuckling. *Shake off the gloom.*

He had his son to consider. No drama right now.

"Papa, what's funny?"

"I'm just laughing at how we are bobbing up and down like little ducks on the waves," he said.

There were 1500 Jews on board the ship. Their passage was financed by a Jewish organization. The American Jewish Distribution Committee paid for their trip, meals, and even a hotel in New York City until they found employment. They paid for all the Jews who came to America through the Truman Act.

They needed a dentist on the ship. Dr. E (Jacob) has always been enterprising and loves to serve his community, so he immediately volunteered. They had a dental office, X-ray machine, chairs, drawers, tools, medicines and everything he would need. Even a dental assistant. He was on call for emergencies, and was requested several times.

Just as the rest of his life had been so unusual, it fits the pattern perfectly that his first real job as a dentist was in the middle of the ocean. He loved the adventure and the challenge of holding instruments steady in the huge up-and-down swings of the ship, and was proud of his work.

As they sailed into New York, they gazed at the Statue of Liberty, Harry's eyes wide as he stood on tiptoe and stared at the giant lady. Jacob told him she was there to welcome them.

Life was more promising now; he had a wife and a little son. They were in America, land of his childhood dreams. Here they could truly make a new beginning.

His dreams eventually were fulfilled, but life was not content to let him slide into home base dirt-free. He was going to be challenged over and over, even with Hitler dead and gone.

CHAPTER 27

America: Living The Dream   1950–1973

*(16) The statue is an icon of freedom and of the United States:
a welcoming signal to immigrants arriving from abroad.
It was a gift to the United States from the people of France.
The head is shown here exhibited at the Paris World's
Fair in 1878. Sculptor, Frédéric Auguste Bartholdi*

IN NEW YORK CITY, JACOB, now Dr. Eisenbach, (Dr. E) was hired at the
Guggenheim Dental Clinic, housed in a 10-story building. Busloads of

indigent children came every 45 minutes for treatment. It was the only place in the whole country that would take a foreign diploma, but he was overjoyed to be living his dream and Papa's, too. Maybe *over*-joyed is inaccurate; it was more like *plenty-deserved*-joyed.

Unfortunately, Irene wasn't happy. "Honey, you have to stop commuting so far to work and then traveling all that way again at night for English lessons. Harry and I never see you." Her mouth was set in a grim line. She had a good point.

Jacob thought fast. "Hmmm. How about if I quit the English class and teach myself? I'll use newspapers, books and the radio. Would that be better?"

"You know it would," she almost purred, pleased with his devotion to her and little Harry.

From that day on, he always had a dictionary with him. In six months he could navigate New York City like a pro. Easy as jumping a fence to avoid Jew-haters with crowbars.

To work anywhere else, though, he had to find a way to attend an American dental school, a giant stumbling block. For a while he tried to just ignore it and enjoy doing dental work at last. But he couldn't ignore it indefinitely. Like the time-worn saying, he was in a place that was nice to visit but they didn't want to live there.

In 1952 they regrouped and moved to Iowa, a beautiful place with a medical and dental school. He was hired by the University of Iowa Hospital to assist in surgery for the Ear, Nose and Throat Department. He learned a great deal but he still wasn't doing dentistry.

He came home with some discouraging news. "Irene, There are 1,000 applicants for every seat in dental school. It's a monumental uphill battle."

"You can beat those odds; you know you can. They don't know who they are dealing with," she chuckled. "You never give up."

It was true: he had fire in him. He didn't – and still doesn't – let hurdles bother him. His desperation and terror at Hitler's hands forged a strength that has rallied him during tough times, all his life.

He applied to the dental school there. The dean and he chatted for twenty minutes, then the dean called in the Senior Faculty Professor to interview him. They gave him no immediate answer, so he went home to try and stay busy while he waited for what could have turned out to be the first of a long line of applications to dental schools. He tried not to think about that.

Then they called him with the news: he was in. He raced into the other room to tell Irene and they shrieked in delight. He picked up Harry and twirled around the room, the little boy in fits of giggles. Finally, they could move forward.

He started as a freshman; they quickly advanced him to the junior class. Very early he showed the skills and abilities that have brought him such success. The dean offered him a residency for oral surgery; he would work up to head of the department and professor. He respectfully declined. It was an opportunity to become an academic, but he knew exactly who he was: he wanted to practice dentistry. No teaching jobs for him.

His first practice was in Cedar Rapids, 25 miles from the University of Iowa. It was a beautiful area and that's as far as they could afford to drive, anyway. Once he established that, it's not hard to imagine how hard he worked. He was the very definition of the word 'motivated'. The practice flourished.

Papa would have been so proud, he mused.

They had two more sons, Mark Charles and David Allen, both healthy and bright. Their family life was everything good about 1950's America. They could have had a TV series; *Leave it to Jacob, or Dr. E Knows Best.*

There was one hitch: Irene's extreme emotional difficulties, which both of them struggled to live with. Meanwhile he became President of their temple and they also attended the theater and traveled. They visited 48 of the 50 states.

In 1973 huge storm clouds gathered again. Irene came in the kitchen one night while he was having tea. The boys were busy doing homework in their rooms.

"I can't stay in Iowa anymore, Jacob. I've suffered too long."

Is it your back?"

"And my arthritis. They will never get better in this cold and humid climate." Her face displayed her frustration; looking older and so tired.

They had discussed this over and over but that night she was at the end of her patience, and he at the end of his grace period. Dr. E put his head in his hands. He would have to sell his practice. He hated to even think of it, but he knew what he had to do. It would mean starting over, at ground zero.

He took a deep breath and looked at her. "Of course we'll move, don't worry." He gave her a little smile. She was visibly relieved; she thought she'd have to use her considerable persuasive powers.

He set about the unnerving business of selling the practice he had worked so hard to build. He looked forward, though, and didn't allow himself to indulge in self-pity. They would be fine.

They moved to sunny Orange County, California. Another nasty old stumbling block cropped up, right on schedule. He was now faced with the California Board exam, which many people couldn't pass the first time. California was very choosy.

"Okay, God, here's where I need you," said Dr. E. "I have trusted you all my life and you've always been there. I am so grateful, but now I need more. This is to support my family, and I know you want me to do that."

God came through like a champ, and so did Dr. E. Between the Almighty's help and Dr. E's inner fire, he passed the test, zippety-smooth.

Hitler's plans for him failed; Adolf gave his all trying to stop Jacob and all the other Jews from breathing, never mind being a dentist. But he lost the battle with Jacob, and with all of the Jews in the end.

It's a beautiful irony. Hitler had fine foods, power and resources. Jacob had nothing, not even his family or enough to eat. He was David to Hitler's Goliath; Jacob won. He didn't shoot Hitler with a sling shot, but he shot him (and so did his fellow Jews) with determination to survive him.

Even those who died survived him by contributing to the momentum that helped Judaism not only thrive, but reclaim Israel after 2,000 years.

Take that, Hitler.

CHAPTER 28

A Busy Career and Life

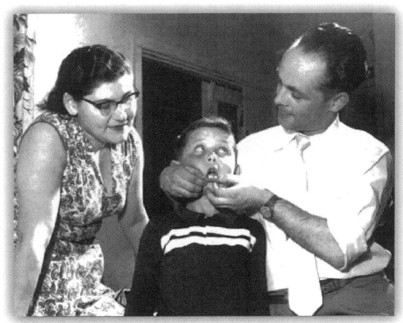

Harry looks a little nervous to have old dad check his teeth.
Mom Irene is sporting a 50's hairdo and cats-eye glasses.
Very trendy for the day. (Dr. Eisenbach's collection)

"DOCTOR," SHE SAID, STEPPING OVER a pile of boards, "a patient has a question on line 2."

A month before his Southern California office was finished Dr. E hired a receptionist. He bought her a desk for the front, and she started work immediately.

There was a sign out front: *Future office of Jacob Eisenbach, DDS.* She made appointments and by the time the office was ready, he was booked for a month. That is *so Jacob.*

It was a huge undertaking to sell out, move and start all over in Southern California. He was offered partnerships but he wanted to start a practice from scratch.

He stays very busy. There have been no sick days for years; instead of the required 25 hours a year of post-graduate work, he does *four times* that many. Of course!

He believes the secret to his longevity involves several qualities. It's important to be optimistic and *love* one's work. Without a passion – work or helping people in some way such as volunteering - nothing drives a person forward.

Second, he believes he has good genes and has always taken care of his health, not fanatically, but with moderation. He does take a lot of vitamin C. He moved on from the nightmare and made the choice to be happy; so far, it's working. He gives more information on how to live a long life is in Appendix 1.

It is very important to lower stress by forgiving people and moving on to the next positive thought. He recently saw a teenage patient who arrived with a swastika tattooed on his hand. One of his dental assistants was appalled. Dr. E shrugged it off. *He's young. He'll learn the important values someday.*

He loves the services he can provide. One day a 56-year-old office manager came to see Dr. E. She was frantic. She had lost all her lower teeth twenty years before.

"I can't live this way," she cried. "When I wear a denture piece it floats around in my mouth."

"That's because there's no bone left to hold it," he said.

"It hurts to bite down. And the worst thing of all is when I am talking with someone, sometimes the piece falls out."

"Don't you worry. We'll take care of this problem," he assured her.

Dentistry has quite a few tricks up its sleeve.

He made computer-assisted implants for her. She looks terrific, even younger, and is one happy patient. Dr. E. was one of the few dentists who could do this at that time.

One thing about him: he lives to serve. Nothing makes him happier than to help someone like this.

He had another bitter pill to swallow. Irene and he were fighting like cats and dogs. After 51 years of marriage.

CHAPTER 29

51-Year Marriage: Another Casualty Of War

Jacob and Irene: party animals!
(Dr. Eisenbach's collection)

ONCE IN THEIR EARLY YEARS together Dr. E was speaking with Irene's cousin. "You know, she is the black sheep of the family," she told him.

"Is that right?" he asked.

Why doesn't this cousin mind her own business?

The woman grinned and nodded her head. "It's true; she is!"

"I guess I prefer black sheep, then," he said, setting his drink down and excusing himself to walk away.

No one knew of her budding mental illness at that time. She wasn't very devoted to the religion, but she did go to temple Friday nights with him and the boys while they were small. Whatever struggles she had, she was always a great mother to their sons.

In the concentration camp, they dreamed about the future. She wanted to be a mother and housewife. They wanted several children, and they would all be smart and beautiful. Her dreams were pretty standard for the day, but she had a definite talent for business that she put to use later in life as a business owner.

In spite of their youthful romantic dreams, when they were married Irene's mood swings couldn't be ignored; she was eventually medically diagnosed with Paranoia. Jacob felt so bad for her. The war and now this. The war had undoubtedly worsened her emotional problems. He and she soldiered on for many years, but sadly, her condition steadily worsened.

She was confrontational and difficult, even with her close friends. Insignificant things became monumental.

The marriage suffered; she thought everything bad that happened was her husband's fault. She could argue like a world-class prosecutor. Dr. E just kept trying to live with it and be optimistic.

Her problems didn't interfere with her work. She owned fabric stores in Iowa which were very profitable, but she worked ridiculously long hours. Later when they lived in California the business bug bit her again and she joined Dr. E in the living room one night for tea.

"Jacob, I've found a great location, and I'd like to put a discount store in there. It's an ideal spot. Would you like to see it?"

She looked at him over the rim of her cup, waiting.

He panicked a little.

Oh, no. All that hard work and stress on her could increase her psychological symptoms.

He chose his words carefully. "I think it would be too much work for you; you will put your whole soul into your store and you will do a great job, but we really don't need the money, Sweetheart." With that bit of sugar on it he hoped for the best.

"You think I would be too exhausted to handle things around here? You don't have much faith in me."

Oh, not good.

"No, no, Irene. That's not it. I just don't want you to hurt your health and I'd like to see you have some fun. You deserve it." He smiled, hoping this would go over better.

She had a couple sips of tea, not answering.

Finally she said "All right, let's put it off for a while."

Thank God, he thought. *That would have put far too much strain on her.*

As it happened, she never did open the discount store.

The first 30 years had been reasonably good, but the last years were so disappointing. Every treatment they tried failed; he took her to the best doctors. The horrors of the war pushed her beyond what she could overcome.

Once they had passed their 50th wedding anniversary, they found themselves filing for divorce in 2,000. It was utterly devastating for Jacob.

No one in his family had ever split up. A Jew might ask: "Why are you getting a divorce? What's the problem? You're adults. Work it out." It's very simple to them, he says.

But not for Irene and Dr. E, dealing with a psychiatric diagnosis like this. They finally came to the point of no return. It wasn't an easy split and tempers got heated.

Jacob felt sad one rainy evening when the divorce was almost final. He sat watching the drops patter down the window and glisten in the street, the kind of weather that makes one sentimental.

He thought bitterly, *I guess our philosophy is 'Wait until you've had your 50th anniversary before you decide if it's going to work'.* He remembered their shared history.

They faced the *Nazis*, met by the *bathroom* and went through the concentration camp horrors together, stayed in the Nazi barracks, rode atop a train all the way home, and combed the ruins in Łódź looking for whatever they could find. They searched in vain for family together. She burned a hole in his pants and they laughed. They had a beautiful double wedding. They snuck over the Polish border in the middle of the night holding hands. They had little Harry in Germany. The three of them sailed to America together over the stormy North Atlantic. They traveled the world. And now they had three sons and two grandchildren.

He so hoped they could at least be friends. Eventually things smoothed out a bit and they became friends again a year before she died on May 15, 2013.

After the divorce, Dr. E decided he didn't want to be alone. He had a lot of living yet to do. After all, he was only 77 years old. He dusted off the old charms and turned his attention to a woman named Shirley, who had previously been a family friend.

She intrigued him; she was president of a large Jewish fundraising organization that provided funds to charities. They went dining and dancing and had many friends they socialized with. She died when Jacob was 80 years old, still not ready to hang up his dancing shoes.

He found himself attracted to Shirley's sister, Bebe. He says she was the 'cutest little 80-year-old angel' he'd ever seen. They spent time together and Bebe told him in 2003 "Now that I have you, I'll never let you go."

They are still together; he lives in Orange County, CA for his business and she lives near Los Angeles. Every Friday afternoon he commutes through LA traffic to see her. Many people half his age would resist driving in that kind of traffic. On Mondays he drives back to Orange County where he lives. When it comes to managing long-distance relationships, younger people have nothing on them!

Read on to find out how Jacob felt when he finally made it to the pyramids.

CHAPTER 30

A Quick Tour Of The World 1950-Present

*(17) Hitler plays tourist at the Eiffel Tower after
conquering the city; Paris, 1940. Dr. Eisenbach
later posed in the same place, but Hitler is
dead and Dr. E is very much alive.*

DR. E HAS TRAVELED THE world, one of his childhood dreams. This is the quick tour for arm-chair travelers.

After his experience being shipped like a side of beef, could he ever ride a train again? Actually, yes. Sometimes he surprises himself how versatile and practical he can be. He says a well-kept and beautiful train is a terrific way to travel, and he did so many times in both America and Europe.

In Yugoslavia, the people were very supportive of Jews but were depressed under communism. The family enjoyed the resort on the sea in southern Yugoslavia, Dubrovnik. Women were topless at the beach, which he enjoyed but -- no surprise -- he wouldn't have wanted Irene doing that.

Sadly, almost all the Jewish community there disappeared during the war; Jacob and family were thrilled to tour the ancient synagogue.

In Hungary, people were different. It had been the base of the very powerful Austro-Hungarian Empire before World War 1. As a result, they had more belief in themselves and were more open, friendly and happier. They were not communist. Budapest was charming and gypsies serenaded people in restaurants with their violins.

They visited Caracas, the capital and largest city of Venezuela, with its tropical/savannah climate. They have modern service companies, banks, malls and a stock exchange. Tall buildings overshadow the old marketplace and historic locations.

The family enjoyed shopping in the open markets. The people were friendly and the Spanish architecture is beautiful, but the country has one of the highest murder rates in the world. The poor neighborhoods covering the hills around the city are said to be dangerous at all times. Dr. E didn't go there, so he had a happy experience.

In China, the emperors used to live in the *Forbidden City*, the earthly counterpart to the celestial city of their deities. They had concubines and lived a lavish life style. People were forbidden to come in or go out without the emperor's permission. Common people living in grinding poverty were forbidden to even look inside as they passed by; they would cut off an offending snooper's head. It's now a beautiful museum, which they enjoyed very much.

The Great Wall of China was a surprise – it is not just a big wall. Walking on top of it, suddenly they found themselves above a whole fortress. They appear regularly along the wall. It's one of the Wonders of the World; 5,500 miles long, it winds over mountains, flat land and deserts and took two thousand years to build.

China has stunning scenery. The people are courteous and friendly. They toured a school and the principal explained that children are taught respect for authority and love of country. It was a communist country but they treated tourists very well.

Dr. E and family have been *down under* twice; they have 150 relatives in Australia, descended from the three cousins, sons of Aunt Esther, who left Europe after the war. (They somehow survived the war in Europe through hiding somewhere and sticking together. Aunt Esther and her daughters were gassed.) The Australians were very gracious to immigrating Jews.

It is the world's 6th largest country by area. It's one of the wealthiest countries in the world. Their culture, life style and language are similar to ours. A big plus: kangaroos and koala bears.

They visited Zurich, Switzerland where he saw the breath-taking majesty of the Alps (but didn't see yodelers on top). He says the people have it so good they don't *ever leave*. They are taken care of from cradle to grave and live long lives. The country leads the other nations of the world with the highest standard of living. The democratic government is very efficient, resulting in prosperity.

Dr. E was in Paris for a week where they took home movies. He stood in front of the Eiffel Tower just like Hitler did, but the good news is he's alive and Adolf isn't.

He found Vienna, Austria to be absolutely beautiful. He thought about the Von Trapps from *Sound of Music* (a true story) and their flight from the Nazis across the mountains. The Nazis had their own ideas about *How to Solve a Problem like Maria*. At least the Von Trapps got away even if they did lose all their stuff.

Egypt was a delight. He *loved* the people; their intelligence, their friendliness and kindness. He has been inside the pyramids *three times*. An awesome sight, the base of the largest pyramid is as long as several city blocks. They arrived by car, rather than camel. To enter, people have to crouch way down. Some passage ways are about three feet high. He wondered: surely people weren't *that* much shorter back then, were they?

Looking at those 5,000-year-old wall paintings he realized he was standing in the very spot where ancient Egyptians stood. Man will go on, millennium after millennium, no matter how people try to destroy each other.

Back in America, he attended the opening of the Holocaust Museum in Washington, D.C. Ronald Reagan gave an emotional 45 minute speech. He was magnificent.

"I would have bombed those railroad tracks," he said. "They wouldn't have had any way to get people to the gas chambers."

If only.

CHAPTER 31

Can You Go Home Again?

*(18) Cheerful German and Slovak soldiers posing with a group
of civilians in Komáńcza, Poland September, 1939. This is
the home town of author Karen's grandfather.*

DR. E DID GO HOME again; he visited Poland forty-five years ago. The country was controlled by communists. They welcomed visitors and their money but their own people couldn't get out. The stores were all boarded up and neglected. It was illegal to own one; the government handled it all, though very poorly. He was sad to realize that the helpful and kind

Russians of the liberation days had to go home and live with *this* poor excuse of a government.

He found his mother's grave, spent time with his memories, seeing her in the kitchen once again and hugging them all four at once. He left a candle and part of his heart behind with her.

He then went to where he lived while growing up; it had been a beautiful 3-bedroom apartment. Now it was all broken down and divided into thirds. Two of them were padlocked, which brought him visions of David, Sam and himself hiding in the ghetto apartment and quaking in fear of the Nazis. He knocked at the third door and a young Polish man answered. He welcomed Dr. E heartily and even asked him to stay for dinner. Polish people have great hearts, he says.

His beautiful, statuesque high school was still open but it was falling into neglect. Their main street had been stately, lined with elegant stores; now they were all boarded up. With no private businesses it was pretty dreary.

The park was still beautiful but nature provided most of that. The people were innocently enjoying the weather; lucky for them, they had no idea what happened right where they were sitting. They had probably never encountered such evil as fellow countrymen using crowbars to beat people into bloody corpses.

He went to see Auschwitz to pay respects to his family. He hated the place. It just gripped him in the heart; he could hardly speak because his throat was so tight. Most of his relatives and his brother Henry died there. He stared at the ovens, the gas chambers, the railroad tracks.

It is now a museum; people toss roses and mementos on those railroad tracks leading to the gate. It's a nightmare that will not end, and it shouldn't. He says we need to remember it to prevent anything even remotely like it from happening again. The two camps he lived in have been torn down, and justly so. Auschwitz is enough, he says.

He did not visit Sam's grave; the town where he was killed and buried was too stark and bitter a place for him. Jacob could not bring himself to see it, but it was a small comfort that Sam at least had a grave. Papa, Henry and Fela didn't even have that.

Where You Go, I go. Sorry, Sam, Bialystock is one place I just cannot go. But I will always love you.

In his home town of Łódź, the youngest Jew was 72. The younger survivors cleared out as soon as possible. There hadn't been a Jewish wedding, a Jewish baby born, or a *Bar Mitzvah* there in 30 years. Before the war 3.5 million Jews lived in Poland; as of 2009, there were only 30-40,000 observant Jews. The government is trying to coax them back, and since the late 1970's it is no longer communist, so maybe they'll succeed.

There's such irony in the communists taking over half of Germany and all of Poland. Many Germans turned a blind eye to the persecution of Jews because they were told, and they believed, Jews promoted communist interests. In fact, quite the opposite. Hitler's slaughter of innocent Jews and the war *Hitler started* opened the door for communism to come right on in.

Dr. E and family took money to Poland with them, but there wasn't much to buy. You could get a meal in a restaurant and rent a hotel room. When they went to dinner, they had a delicious 6- or 7-course meal which cost the equivalent of 50 American cents. Communists controlled all prices. In Hungary, non-communist, the same meal cost the equivalent of 12 American dollars.

He says one of the light, fresh-air feelings in America is the freedom to go anywhere. In communist countries, you have to ask permission to change your residence, or even get yourself around. You need identification with you at all times. Speech is not free; gathering in groups is risky. You live in a virtual prison.

He found cousin Lolek in Poland and visited him while there. He later visited him again in Israel. He also found his best friend from childhood, Jack Sieradski, and visited him. Jack and his family had somehow avoided the ghetto; Jacob doesn't remember how, but they had to have been in hiding. Jack worked in textiles and later came to New York.

Meanwhile, what became of the tiny country of Israel which was established after the Holocaust? How did it survive the hostility of the countries surrounding it? Read on to find out; this tiny country has the heart of a lion.

CHAPTER 32

This Little Lamb Isn't So Meek

Dr. E and son David at the
Wailing Wall in Israel.
(Dr. Eisenbach's collection)

DR. E SAYS JEWS GOT *one special gift from the Holocaust*: the State of Israel. He loves it and has been there ten times. The annihilation they suffered gave them enough anger to reclaim their country after 2,000 years. Hitler energized these people into finally taking action.

Ancient Rome forced them out; it had conquered Palestine in 63 BCE with four legions. Jews fought back, but the Great Jewish Revolt in 66 CE failed and the Jewish temple in Jerusalem was destroyed.[4]

While in exile, faithful Jews shared the word of God all over the world. They taught the pagan King of Hawaii about God and that He is the *only* God. That belief, monotheism, was started by the first Jew 4,000 years ago. His name was Abraham.

Israel passed the *Law of Return* which says a Jew can come to Israel from anywhere in the world and be a citizen *that day.*

When it was established in 1948 Israel was tiny; there were only 600,000 Jews. It was a little lamb with wolves circling it, licking their chops. There were 100 million Arabs who didn't appreciate them being there. Furthermore, they were going to do something about it: wipe Israel off the map immediately.

The poor little lamb had no weapons. There were no rifles, no airplanes. But there were many people the world over who cared. They smuggled in weapons. Even airplanes, though *that* must have been a challenge. America got in on this too.

The world was astonished; Israel survived the attacks of the Six-Day War. They battled the neighboring states of Egypt (United Arab Republic at the time), Jordan and Syria.

Other countries offered to help, but the spunky little country said "We're okay. We've got this."

People backed off, but they worried *Look at the odds. Israel is outnumbered many times over.*

Israel found out the hours the United Arab Republic Army kept; what time their pilots slept. At that exact hour, they dropped laser-guided bombs, one for each plane. The Arab Republic's air force was quickly destroyed, one reason the war only lasted six days.

---

4 First Jewish–Roman War. (2014, May 31). In *Wikipedia, The Free Encyclopedia.* Retrieved 18:18, July 16, 2014, from http://en.wikipedia.org/w/index.php?title=First_Jewish%E2%80%93Roman_War&oldid=610898752

Israelis showed tremendous valor in battle. At one point, men placed their bodies over barbed wire and let their fellow soldiers vault over them.

As a result of the threat surrounding the little country, in the war Israel seized the *Gaza Strip, Sinai Peninsula, West Bank of the Jordan River, East Jerusalem, and the Golan Heights. Its territory tripled.*

The political importance was immense. Israel proved it could and *would* do strategic strikes that could change the balance in the area, if necessary.

Yitzhak Rabin, fifth Prime Minister of Israel, said the reason for the victory was that Jews knew they had to win or the result would be annihilation.

Hitler had given them the push they needed.

Now the country is populated by six million, the same number of Jews killed in the Holocaust. It's an industrial country; there are thousands of entrepreneurships and it's strong in science and medical research.

It's a wonderful country, he says. There are a lot of business owners and technological advances. The *Hadassah* Medical Center in Israel is a world-class hospital that attracts patients from all over the world. They cured the King of Saudi Arabia of pancreatic cancer and he donated millions of dollars to the hospital. Patients don't have to be Jewish; they will treat everyone, even their enemies.

The people are bound together by a steely determination. *"We will be strong. We might forgive, but we will never forget. There will NEVER be another Holocaust."*

CHAPTER 33

A Hard-Knock Education: Where's The Meaning?

(19) <u>Warsaw Uprising</u>.
*This woman is dangling above the street, trying to escape. When
she drops to the ground, the Nazis will shoot her.*

DR. E WAS SPEAKING AT a junior high school recently. He always welcomes
the opportunity.

Taking the microphone, he greeted the students and introduced
himself. He asked "Have any of you heard the Holocaust didn't happen?
That it's a hoax?"

A few hands went up. Others looked around, as if they weren't sure what was expected of them.

"Let me show you a few pictures," he said, using the projector to flash images of his family on the screen. The children leaned forward to get a good look, particularly at Fela, such a pretty girl.

"They were killed by Hitler. Some in camps, others on the street. My uncle was murdered in his own home. My little brother," he pointed to Henry's picture, "was taken out of the hospital and thrown in the back of a Nazi truck."

The children's mouths fell open. "He was put in a pile of sick people, stacked up like herring in a barrel."

You could hear a pin drop in the auditorium.

"Then they took them to Auschwitz where they were all killed by poisonous gas in a sealed room, designed to look like a shower. Afterward they were incinerated like trash."

He waited for that to sink in. The children never saw anything like this in their own lives. Sure, in the movies or on the news, but this man was real flesh and blood, standing there with pictures of his murdered family.

Were They Just A Puff Of Smoke?

He put down the clicker. "Now when you hear 'There never was a Holocaust' what does that mean? My family just disappeared into thin air? They were just my imagination? A puff of smoke?"

He paused for dramatic effect. "The answer is yes, they were a puff of smoke. After Hitler gassed them and then burned their bodies in a big oven."

The students were mesmerized. They left their cell phones untouched and stared at him. He told them what it was like to see people beaten to death with crowbars, to live in the ghetto, to starve, to receive no medical treatment, to have one family member at a time taken. To lose all your possessions. To have airplanes fire at helpless people on the road.

He finished his speech urging them to be watchful. "Guard your precious minds against intolerance, discrimination, and hatred. Don't let anyone corrupt your thinking. This is a wonderful country and I'm so grateful to be living here where we can worship as we like, and be of any race whatever."

When he finished, he got a standing ovation from kids who usually only pay attention to current songs, social media and their latest crush. It thrilled him; not just some polite applause. A *standing ovation* from these kids.

They lined up and he gave them the microphone. They surprised him with insightful questions. A boy said his grandparents (or possibly great-grandparents) were killed by Hitler. Every time Jacob can pass along what he's learned, it enriches his life, too.

He stays socially connected. He has many friends and goes to lunch or dinner with them. He is great friends with a Rabbi and a Catholic priest.

Anger and bitterness have no place in his heart because they destroy health and happiness. He moved on from the nightmare and made the choice to be happy; so far, it's working.

AUSCHWITZ TATTOOS: FLAGS OF VICTORY

Dr. E's philosophy keeps him healthy and optimistic. It's time to get past all the morbidity, he says. There was a documentary about concentration camp tattoos filmed in Israel. An American audience of survivors didn't react well to it. Dr. E was the speaker afterwards and suggested they regard the tattoos as flags of victory over Hitler. They are alive; Hitler isn't.

"Years ago I realized a person needs to have a certain degree of contentment with their station in life. After WWII, we had won. Hitler died and is ashes now just like his victims. We live in America, the best country that ever existed. Jews also have our homeland of Israel. I try to be conscious of my blessings and remain grateful."

What would have happened if leaders and citizens of other countries stood up against Hitler right from the start? There were a few countries that actually did.

Brave Souls Who DEFIED Hitler

After he occupied Denmark, leaving the king on the throne, he ordered all the Jews to wear the Star of David. The king told him *NO*, but Hitler was not about to be ignored.

"All right, then, we'll all wear stars, myself included. We are all Jews in Denmark," the king said. Dr. E loves that.

The gesture was appreciated by the Jews, but they were not out of danger. Germany took over the government of Denmark after its members resigned, protesting Hitler's actions. He promptly ordered all Danish Jews to be deported (and gassed).

Sweden came to the rescue, offering asylum to Danish Jews; the Danes responded immediately. Many citizens came to the aid of Jews. Over 99% of Danish Jews survived the Holocaust, evacuated to Sweden on fishing boats.

Hitler allowed Sweden to remain neutral for the time being; he had his hands full at the moment. In the end, he never had the chance to occupy Sweden, though he definitely planned to. Only seven other European nations were able to officially remain neutral for the entire war: Ireland, Portugal, Spain, Andorra, Liechtenstein, Vatican City and Switzerland.[5]

Hitler occupied Italy, land of the hated Mussolini, another ally he betrayed. Now Hitler was up against a man like himself. Once again, one of Dr. E's favorite anecdotes:

Hitler demanded Mussolini turn over the Jews. *Il Duce* scoffed. "We have no Jews here; only Italians."

---

5 Neutral powers during World War II. (2014, July 11). In *Wikipedia, The Free Encyclopedia*. Retrieved 18:40, July 16, 2014, from http://en.wikipedia.org/w/index.php?title=Neutral_powers_during_World_War_II&oldid=A616492651

Of course that did not deter Hitler a bit. When it came to a pee-ing contest between Mussolini and Hitler, the guy with the funny mustache won.

Catholics Protect And Save Jews

So the citizens of Italy took it upon themselves to protect Jews. *The Catholic Church* had a large network of safe hideouts in convents and religious houses, especially in Rome.

Imagine for a minute the cooperation this involved. Many Catholics at the time believed Jews were not going to heaven because they rejected Christ. In spite of that, they saved many Jews and even hid them in their sacred *convents*. It's a testament to the basic goodness of most people. Doctors, town clerks, farmers, even *smugglers* offered help to the persecuted. Anti-fascist resistance groups gave them shelter, too.

Individuals Who Fought Back

Dr. E is touched by the actions of Raoul Wallenberg. He was a compassionate man from Sweden, ambassador to Hungary. He issued thousands of visas and Jews became instant Swedish citizens in a neutral country, where Hitler couldn't touch them.

This one principled man saved tens of thousands of people. In 1945 he was detained by the Soviet government and subsequently disappeared. The mystery remains unsolved, but it's not hard to guess what happened. The real mystery is *why*? Mr. Wallenberg and Russia were supposed to be on the same side, against Hitler.

Another man Dr. E admires is former Japanese ambassador to Lithuania, Chiune Sugihara.[6] He also couldn't stand the cruelty to Jews. Though Japan was *allied with Hitler*, he asked for permission from his

---

6 Chiune Sugihara. (2014, July 6). In *Wikipedia, The Free Encyclopedia*. Retrieved 18:33, July 16, 2014, from http://en.wikipedia.org/w/index.php?title=Chiune_Sugihara&oldid=615850514

government for 6,000 visas for Jews. The government laughed at him. He issued them anyway.

The Jews arrived in Japan and escaped to other Asian countries. Smart move. Sugihara was demoted and died in poverty and obscurity; he was lucky not to be executed. Today he's a hero in Japan and honored as a great humanitarian. Happily, Jacob has met many kind people from Japan here in America.

Dr. E cautions, if you hear '*So many people hate the Jews*' it's not true. There were many beautiful people that came to the aid of the Jews during the war; many risked their own lives, including many Polish people. Two brothers hid a family in a hole in the ground and fed them for a year.

Golda Meir, Prime Minister of Israel, said Israeli soldiers fight to defend their family and their country, without hatred.

One of the finest things a human being can accomplish is to turn an enemy into a friend. Anwar Sadat, President of Egypt thirty years ago, couldn't win by fighting with Israel. He decided to make peace and went to Jerusalem to speak to the Israeli Parliament (Knesset). He changed his attitude from hatred to friendship and they responded. The peace they have is still holding. Sadly, he was assassinated by his enemies.

So Many Countries (Including Us) Had Foggy Brains

When the Japanese attacked America, the US started creating armaments. According to Dr. E, the U.S. should have been active in Europe earlier. It seems America was guilty of the same foggy brain common at the time regarding Hitler.

He says "America should have done it six months or a year earlier, but once the Yanks were in there, they did a great job".

He is grateful for what America provides; we have plenty of food, but he doesn't throw out *any* food unless he absolutely has to, a common aftermath of starvation. He *loves* to go grocery shopping, with all the varieties of food arrayed for the shopper's pleasure. Most people don't think about it, but this is an absolute privilege.

The pictures of Dr. E and his family in the early days were given to him by his cousins in Buenos Aires, Argentina. He feels fortunate to have them because the Nazis made fast work of any such mementos in Jewish homes.

Read on to find out why Churchill was playing with balloons in the last months of the war.

Churchill's Balloons   1944

(20) *Let's get them with our balloons! British female
military auxiliaries handle a barrage balloon.*

ONE OF DR. E'S FAVORITE stories is about Churchill's balloons. *Operation
Outward* was his answer to Hitler's *vengeance weapon*, a new long-range bal-
listic missile. He planned to obliterate England with it.

Female military auxiliaries were responsible for launching the balloons. They were unmanned and carried either a trailing wire designed to damage high-voltage power lines, or an incendiary device for setting fires in Germany's heartlands. With these, Churchill forced Germany to assign people to fire watching, which took away from their war effort.

The balloons were making their mark. Churchill said the value of harassment on German air defenses alone justified the program. It cost the Germans more to destroy each balloon than it cost England to make it, to Churchill's delight.

As Churchill hoped, the balloons caused forest fires in Germany. The high mark of the campaign was when a balloon caused the destruction by fire of the German power station at Böhlen.

Unfortunately there were a few mishaps. Sometimes the wind pushed the balloons the wrong direction. A balloon knocked out electrical lighting on the railway in Laholm, Sweden, and a pair of trains collided.

The balloons were capable of turning on their master, too. Sometimes balloons wandered with the wind back into England. Once a balloon knocked out the electricity in Ipswich.

In the closing days of the war, 1300 missiles were fired on London killing almost 3000, but did not achieve the total wipe-out Hitler demanded. He had briefed his staff, *"We may go down but we will take the world with us."*

He had a good run at it, but he certainly didn't take the world down with him. Although his victims numbered in the multi-millions, the only one he actually took down *with* him, sitting right beside him, was poor naïve and devoted little Eva Braun, his long-patient mistress. They committed suicide together. She had never discussed politics with him, or any of the elite; she was mostly kept in the dark. She loved the man, not the Nazi.

Another story Dr. E likes is about the role *storks* played in the war. The birds migrating from the Netherlands to South Africa delivered not *babies*, but messages tied to their legs. *"Save us. The Nazis are killing us all."* What a chilling discovery that must have been.

On the lighter side, one might imagine the birds with messages strutting around, all proud of themselves. One of the rare humorous moments in WWII history.

———❦———

This is the last chapter, although several appendices follow with information on Dr. Eisenbach's family and his tips on living a long and productive life. Appendix 2 has some interesting facts the world found out after the war.

If his story helps or inspires you in any way, Dr. E is delighted and the two years we spent on this book will have served its purpose.

Afterward

L – R: *Son Harry, Jacob, son Mark Charles, wife Irene, son David*
(Dr. Eisenbach's collection)

JACOB'S GREATEST BLESSINGS AND JOY are his children, grandchildren, and great grandchildren.

Ten years after Harry was born, they had Mark Charles. Dr. E was delighted; a man can't have too many sons. Irene didn't appear to miss having a daughter; she was always devoted to the boys.

A few years later their third son, David, was born. By this time, Dr. E was a little more relaxed in the waiting room. As he sipped some coffee, he mused *Should I do like Papa and encourage them to be doctors?* No. They would make him proud whatever career they chose. It turns out one of them did become a doctor; Harry, their little sailor.

Harry has a charming French wife Frederique; they live in Malibu, 'the Bu' as some residents call it. They have a handsome and very successful son, Ben, who has three children, Dr. E's great-grandchildren. Boys Chase and Asher and a baby girl named Anderson Rose. Ben's wife Robyn is a lovely woman and good mother.

Their second son Mark Charles, a gifted businessman, died a few years ago of a heart attack at age 51. People are not supposed to outlive their children. Even though Jacob survived everything he has no protection from the *'slings and arrows of outrageous fortune'*, as Shakespeare penned in *Hamlet.*

Sarah, Mark's lovely dark-haired daughter, as of July 2014 was an editor for a law book publisher in Orange County near Jacob. She also was a newlywed and Dr. E enjoyed attending the wedding.

Third son David Allen is a tall, hard-working business owner. His first marriage ended with no children, and when she heard this, his USC college sweetheart Rika came here from Japan and married him. He helped her raise her daughter Amy. As a father 'on a scale of 1 to 10' Amy says "he's a 200".

Jacob's sweetheart, Bebe, has a helper, Norma De Jesus, who cleans the house, cooks for them and looks after Bebe around the clock.

God is still producing miracles in Dr. E's life. Recently Bebe repeatedly said "I'm going to visit my mother now." (Her mother died years ago.) She was unable to relax.

"Bebe, be calm. Listen to this." Norma sat with her and put her hand on Bebe's head; she read some Bible passages. An amazing peace settled over Bebe that lasted all day. Jacob believes God looks after details like this for him, because he's had so many struggles along the way.

Dr. E keeps in touch with survivors through clubs and organizations for them.

He and Bebe see friends occasionally from a survivor group made up of people from *Łódź*. Weekdays Dr. E is busy socially in Orange County, going out to lunch or dinner.

Their son David began a genealogy for them, but didn't discover much because the records were gone. The Nazis used birth, death and marriage records for cigarette papers. Even their family history turned to ashes thanks to Hitler. He did find out that his ancestors may have come from Romania.

He wants this book to reach people who believe they are alone in their pain. He is thinking of all of you. You don't have to feel hopeless; you can find meaning in life, no matter if your prison is a bad marriage, a physical handicap, a lack of education, mental issues like depression or addictions, or the tragic loss of one or more family members. All these can be overcome and you can succeed at work you love, making a contribution that matters.

All in all, life has been very good, he says, his eyes sparkling with optimism. See Appendix 1 for his secrets to long life.

Dr. E's Secrets To Long Life And Productivity

*Keep a sense of humor. First wife Irene, my granddaughter Sarah and I,
with a distant relative who looks so serious. (Dr. Eisenbach's collection)*

I CAN ONLY SHARE MY own experience, but I have followed these principles
all my life and survived the worst imaginable difficulties. I work full time
and never take sick days. I don't need to. I'm not only healthy, but I'm
happy as well.

Genetics undoubtedly play a part in longevity. Still, whatever your heredity, you can maximize your lifespan. And when you reach your senior citizenship, it is important to do more than wake up and breathe in and out every day. You want a vigorous enjoyment of life, right? I'll bet if you're reading this, you're willing to make some changes, if necessary. Here's how I do it.

My unique background in the concentration camps has contributed to my longevity. You undoubtedly have not had experience in a prison camp, but you may have faced much adversity. The terrible struggle actually made me stronger and I believe has contributed to my long and active life.

Persecution by the Nazis led me to accept the ancient concept of "Blessed are the peacemakers" and I have spent my life trying to be a peacemaker and contribute to society. This reduces stress which is very important to healthy living. It helps to prevent stroke, heart attack and similar stress-induced illnesses.

MENTAL / SPIRITUAL

1) *Have a positive attitude.* Perhaps it was God-given, or maybe the influence of my parents, but I was blessed with optimism from a youthful age. It's not easy to remain positive when you are persecuted by Nazis, but what I couldn't do myself, God supplied. Also, my parents, especially my mother influenced me, even after she died; I drew strength from her throughout everything. Additionally, Sam and I relied on each other and our friends.

Once I was back in the land of the living, life didn't suddenly become a bed of roses. There were plenty of serious difficulties, but I was determined not to let my attitude slide into bitterness and pessimism. I believe this may be the most critical of all my secrets. Do your best to develop a philosophy of the goodness of life and mankind; I've found spirituality makes that a lot easier.

Keep up *hope*. No matter how dark the clouds become, there will be a time when the sun will come out again. When you are at the bottom of the pit, you cannot go down any further. The only way is up.

2) *Believe in the basic goodness of human beings.* If you think about it, you will see that killers and thieves are in the minority. They make the headlines, while the huge majority of people lead ordinary lives and aren't called to our attention.

Notice when a stranger lends you a hand, or when a child offers to help you in some way. Be aware that neighbors watch out for you; often strangers will put themselves in danger to help you if you are in peril. Most people are moved to kindness and love towards animals, whether they see a baby penguin, a new puppy, an eagle, a dolphin or a silly old turtle lumbering along.

Even Hitler's killing squads were tormented by the evil they were doing and many committed suicide after the war. One of their commandants spoke about this.

At the time of the massacres, sometimes Heinrich Himmler had to pump them up to do it, and they were more or less brainwashed by the Hitler cult, buying into the idea that they were doing the right thing. Hard to imagine, but that seems to be what drove them. It's probably safe to say in a Germany without Hitler, those men would never have done the kinds of things they did.

3) *Believe in God, the creator of everything.* A powerful way to find God is simply to ask Him for help or strength and then watch Him at work. You may be surprised at the small size of prayers He will answer, not just the big ones. Is He really there? Imagine being given the parts of a bug and asked to assemble it and have it

crawl across a table. Now imagine being asked to create a dinosaur or a blue whale.

4) *Enjoy your work.* This is fairly well understood these days, but it's worth repeating. If you hate your job, it takes a toll on your body. Try to find something you love to do. If you are able, train for it. If you think you're too old for that, you can always find some volunteer work you enjoy to enhance your life and the lives of others. If you have children and have no time for that, it's okay; you have a few years yet ahead of you! Perhaps right now they are meant to be your purpose. Enjoy them while you can.

5) *Have a good social life.* This is believed to be critical to people's well-being. So if you don't have anything happening there, find something you can join. Make some new friends. Get to know your neighbors. Join a church, synagogue or mosque. Take a dance class or join a hiking club.

   If you are a senior, there are likely plenty of opportunities to get involved in something in your community. I have a very busy social life, because it's important to me. I get out there and do things. Take seminars, go out to dinner with friends, drive to Los Angeles each weekend to visit my angel. It's never too late.

   I am good friends with a rabbi and a Catholic priest. The priest is a patient of mine and we have developed an amazing friendship. I take him out to lunch every five years. Author Karen thinks this is hilarious. Well, I *am* very busy!

6) *Keep stress down as much as possible.* How to do that is the subject of many good books. Meditation is excellent. Takin leisurely walks, or even more vigorous walks is wonderful. Nature has a way of calming and soothing people. Most people love the beach. Water seems to be connected to our most basic needs for security and tranquility.

Have a pet. Simply holding a pet and stroking its fur will lower your blood pressure. Also, eating good food is soothing. Just don't treat your stress by drinking too much or smoking, obviously. That only increases the problem.

7) *Build a loving family.* If you were born into a large family, you have a number of people to enjoy; some will be closer than others, but at least you have a lot of options! People with very small families or those, like myself, who lost their family will need to build a new one through marriage or perhaps adoption.

If you have grandchildren, enjoy them as much as you can. They will grow up as fast as your own children did.

If children are not for you, or you are alone in your senior years, then you can develop a few solid friendships that feel like family. You must be proactive. They likely won't come to your door and invite you to blend into their lives. Perhaps in certain communities they will; but if not, see the comments above on building a social life.

8) *"I never met a man I didn't like,"* Will Rogers said. (We assume he never met a woman he didn't like, either.) His philosophy is wonderful, however, because it benefits you much more than the people you meet and like. You will have more energy and happiness when you find the good in people.

9) *Optimism and hope are extremely important in longevity.* If you have cancer, there are excellent sources of support where you learn how to live with it and be happy. The emphasis is on *living*, not dying. Some optimistic people beat cancer or live with it for twenty more years than they were given by doctors.

10) *Believing in life after death will go a long way in avoiding fear of death.* Ever since primitive societies, men have been reporting near death experiences (NDE's) which is why all cultures believe in Heaven, Nirvana, Happy Hunting Grounds, Valhalla, or something similar. We have a lot more NDE's these days with our

advanced medical techniques of reviving people, so you may even know someone who has a story to tell.

Author Karen had a fourth-grade student who had died the year before in a drowning accident. He was finally revived in the hospital, and when he returned he described sitting in a big swing in the sky with an angel, watching the activities in the hospital emergency room. He was able to describe what happened around him while he was 'gone'. He spoke of the angel touching his forehead and sending him back to his body with a 'bang'. This sudden return is consistent with many stories given by NDE'ers.

Karen says he was a sweet little guy with no propensity for lying or bragging. His words were "I'm not afraid of dying; I've been dead and it's WONDERFUL."

PHYSICAL

You may have expected this to come first. I placed it after the mental and spiritual aspects because I believe mind and spirit can diminish problems in the body or even prevent them from happening.

1) *Regular exercise builds good blood circulation and enhances overall health.* It helps control weight, lowers blood pressure, improves mood, fights depression, keeps you younger. What you don't use, you lose! Plus, you can improve your social life through an exercise class, walking group, dance class, or golf.

2) *Eat a healthy diet. I am not an extremist and believe in moderation.* I enjoy pizza and other tasty things, but overall I eat a balanced and healthy diet. We are what we eat, chemically at least.

3) *Keep your weight down.* I don't mean obsessively; you don't need to add stress to your life by writing down every calorie you eat. Simplify it and eat when you are hungry. If you aren't so hungry, take a couple bites and stop. Eat your favorite

foods, paying attention to your hunger level. Stop when you're comfortable.

It's important not to deny yourself foods you love. Why would you want to live a long time with boring food at every meal? Enjoy eating! It adds to the gusto in life. Just make sure you are not ignoring what your body tells you. If you have an eating disorder, get help for it now so you can enjoy living (and eating).

4) *Take supplements, especially 500-1000 mg. of Vitamin C daily.* Read about Dr. Linus Pauling, Nobel Laureate winner whose work with Vitamin C so greatly influenced our lives.

5) *Get 7 to 8 hours of sleep a night.* Some people go on four hours, and perhaps they are the exception that proves the rule. For most of us, however, 7 to 8 hours is where we function best. Lack of sleep impairs you mentally and lowers your resistance to disease.

6) *Have a regular physical exam even if you feel good.*

7) Finally, *teeth,* one of my favorite subjects. *Take good care of your teeth and practice prevention of gum disease and tooth decay.* Good health in this area will add to the quality of your life through your continued ability to eat normally, and be free of pain and suffering, not to mention dental bills. Also dental problems can lead to physical problems in other parts of the body.

There you have my philosophy of living a long, healthy life. My fondest hope is that you are able to get a bit of help from this. I had to work hard to learn it all!

On the right is my ladylove, Bebe. The dark-haired girl is Janet, a family friend. (Dr. Eisenbach's collection)

God Bless You,
Jacob Eisenbach, D.D.S. June 2015

Author's Note
What The World Found Out After The War

⎯⎯⎯ ◆ ⎯⎯⎯

MANY FASCINATING THINGS TURNED UP in my research. The information is not a part of Dr. E's personal story, so I've included the most astonishing things I learned about Hitler's Germany in this appendix.

<u>DID GERMAN CHILDREN REALLY HAVE TO PUT THEIR LIVES ON THE LINE?</u>

YES, in defending Berlin. Fearless in combat, the boys sprang from behind trees and had to be shot or they would toss a grenade at an allied tank. Our soldiers were shocked at how tough these youths were; many of them took bullets for Hitler's cause.

They promised loyalty to Hitler until death and far too many kept that promise. Allied soldiers found numerous young boys who committed suicide rather than be captured. No doubt they looked at the little corpses and shook their heads. *What kind of monster sends children to war?*

Even girls were using anti-aircraft guns right alongside the boys.

A Hitler Youth was filmed playing with live ammunition and a tank. "This is more fun than school," he said, smiling. His rude awakening was on its way.

HOW THE KILLING SQUADS WERE EMOTIONALLY ABLE TO DO IT

In spite of how ruthless they look on film, it wasn't easy; they paid a price. Sometimes the SS men on assassination teams became so disheartened Heinrich Himmler would stand up in his army vehicle and give them a pep talk. He told them to do this for Germany. Sort of an early version of JFK's speech: *Ask not what your country can do for you...*

They continued with the murders, but a number of them later committed suicide and some became mentally ill. An SS Commander reported this after the war.

HITLER MEETS HIS MAKER (What a meeting that must have been)

When the time came, (soon after he praised, and then sent the final group of kids into battle) Hitler and Eva went into his private room and closed the door. They had been married just 40 hours.

She was much younger than he, but remained totally enraptured by him. The new Mrs. Hitler wore his favorite blue dress and had her hair and make-up done exquisitely. They sat on a couch together; she had a slender, athletic build, and had her legs drawn up and feet tucked under in a demure fashion. Those left of his inner circle were waiting outside, straining to hear. Ten minutes of muffled conversation played out inside the room. Then a shot rang out.

When the group entered, her head was resting against Hitler, having taken cyanide and quickly died. He had put a poison capsule in his mouth, then shot himself in the head.

GOOD-BYE, MR. GOEBBELS

Magda Goebbels is said to have killed her beautiful children then, not wanting them to grow up with the terrible stigma of an arch-criminal father. It is thought either a Nazi dentist or Hitler's doctor injected them with morphine to make them sleep. Helga Suzanne, 12 years old by then, was skeptical about the shot. When they were asleep, Magda, possibly aided by the dentist/doctor, put cyanide between their teeth to crush the capsules. Helga's face was significantly bruised; she apparently woke and put up quite a struggle.[7]

Then Joseph and Magda Goebbels killed themselves. It is thought that they followed Hitler's example; he shot himself and his wife took poison. Any Nazi honchos remaining fled the scene. Secretaries and other low-level personnel also escaped at this time, all of whom were pursued by interrogators; many were jailed for a time.

THE END OF HEINRICH HIMMLER

He was in British custody, having approached them trying to negotiate a deal. Needless to say, there was no deal. Instead, he was arrested. He swallowed a cyanide capsule, killing himself instantly before they could even interrogate him.

His wife and beloved daughter struggled for years to overcome the stigma of being his family.

HOW WERE THE GERMAN PEOPLE FORCED TO PAY FOR WHAT HITLER DID?

Many people in the Allied countries felt that the Germans should have stopped Hitler. Furious with the Germans, *especially* after they saw the concentration camps and piles of skeletons, the Allies weren't in a giving mood.

Germans struggled in their bombed out cities. The Allies walked them through the concentration camps and made the horrified and shamed people, young and old alike, look at all the emaciated bodies and stare into the ovens. If a German backed away from a room of bodies, an Allied soldier would shove him in and make him look. Some of these camps were close to populated areas. Allies thought there was no *way* these people didn't know what was going on all around them.

---

7 Joseph Goebbels. (2014, July 15). In *Wikipedia, The Free Encyclopedia*. Retrieved 18:03, July 16, 2014, from http://en.wikipedia.org/w/index.php?title=Joseph_Goebbels&oldid=617092559

Jews were fed by a Jewish organization, but three million 'Arian' Germans starved to death while the Allies looked the other way. After that, the U. S. became uneasy. Starving them might put the Germans right back where they were when they accepted Hitler's leadership. The Allies didn't want *that*. They began feeding them and tried to assist them in building something positive from the ruins, as everyone's psychic wounds began to heal.

DEATH TRAINS

Often had 60 'cattle wagons' with 130 people in each; 7,800 people per train. They once rounded up 15,000 small children and elders from Jacob's ghetto and sent them to their deaths. One has to wonder: were those kids excited to see the train, eager to ride it? It remains one of the hardest things to comprehend; how could they *do this* to their fellow man? These victims were *not cattle*.

WHO FINANCED THE WAR?

Resources taken from Jews financed 30% of Hitler's war activities. What a surprise.

HOW MANY JEWS SURVIVED IN POLAND?

Of 3.5 million Jews in Poland 200,000 survived, roughly 1 in 20. Only 800 Jews from the original 180,000 remained in the Łódź Ghetto on the day of liberation by the Soviets, January 19, 1945.

Tributes To Dr. Jacob Eisenbach: A Man For All Seasons

---⦿⦿⦿---

United States Federal and State Awards

CERTIFICATE OF CONGRESSIONAL RECOGNITION 6/14/2015
United States Congress
For: World War II Concentration Camp Survivor
Bravery and Perseverance

CALIFORNIA LEGISLATURE, ASSEMBLY: CERTIFICATE OF
RECOGNITION   6/18/2015
For: World War II Concentration Camp Survivor
Guardian and Protector of Freedom

STATE OF CALIFORNIA SENATE: CERTIFICATE OF
RECOGNITION
ORANGE COUNTY REPUBLICAN WOMEN FEDERATED
6/18/2015
For: World War II Concentration Camp Survivor

Personal Testimonials

It is a great honor for me to be asked to add a few words about the distinguished career of Doctor Jacob Eisenbach. He has been my dentist since I first came to Anaheim Hills in July 1976. In the numerous times we have met for social outings he has always been a most kind, caring and wonderful professional man. I have never encountered a doctor that is his equal in kindness, competence and efficiency.

Sharing his life story with me caused us to become real friends and deepened my admiration for him and those who endured similar struggles. He lives his life according to the best Jewish and Christian principles which is an example and incentive to all of us to do likewise.

Dr. Eisenbach, may you always have laughter to cheer you, those you love near you, and all your heart might desire.

Father Seamus A. Glynn
Retired Pastor, San Antonio De Padua del Canon Catholic Church, Anaheim Hills, CA

DR. EISENBACH HAS A RARE kind of courage. To overcome the Holocaust, come to America and start over is an inspiration to all of us. So many who endured the tragedy of the Nazi regime and all the attendant suffering let it be the determining factor in their lives, inhibiting their accomplishments.

Dr. Eisenbach rose above it; he came to this country and has succeeded remarkably.

Rabbi David Eliezrie
North County Chabad Center, Yorba Linda, CA

Photo Credits

———✦———

(1) _Jews from the Łódź ghetto are loaded onto freight trains for deportation_. Placed in Public Domain, _Courtesy of the National Museum of American Jewish History. Photo #02_

(2) _Adolf Hitler, Joseph Goebbels, Tochter, 1933. Image provided to Wikimedia Commons by the German Federal Archive (Deutsches Bundesarchiv) as part of a cooperation project. Accession Number Bild 183-2004-1202-500, Attribution: Bundesarchiv, Bild 183-2004-1202-500 / CC-BY-SA. Licensed under Creative Commons Attribution-Share Alike 3.0 Germany license. Photographer unknown. Courtesy of Wikipedia, Wikimedia Commons._

(3) _Children of Joseph Goebbels, Christmas 1937, Provided to Wikimedia Commons by the German Federal Archive (Deutsches Bundesarchiv) as part of a cooperation project. Photographer: Wagner. Accession number: Bild 183-C17887. Attribution: Bundesarchiv, Bild 183-C17887 / Wagner / CC-BY-SA 3.0. Licensed: under Creative Commons Attribution-Share Alike 3.0 Germany license. Permission is granted to share, copy, distribute, and transmit the work; to remix or adapt the work._

(4) _1939 Nazis Entering Łódź, Poland_. Public Domain _Poland, and U.S.A; Courtesy of United States. Holocaust Memorial Museum Archives_

(5) *German and Jewish police guard an entrance to the Łódź Ghetto*. Released to public domain by United States Holocaust Memorial Museum. The right to use this work is granted to anyone for any purpose, without any conditions, unless such conditions are required by law.

(6) *Children Being Sent to the Chelmo Death Camp*; Source: USHMM website (United States Holocaust Memorial Museum). Released to the public domain by the United States Holocaust Memorial Museum. Courtesy of United States Holocaust Memorial Museum.

(7) *Chaim Rumkowski, Chairman of the Council of Jewish Elders. Rumkowski, JPG*; Courtesy of Wikimedia Commons. Listed as public domain on the USHMM website. If this is not legally possible, the right to use this work is granted to anyone for any purpose, without any conditions, unless such conditions are required by law.

(8) *Warsaw Ghetto Uprising Poland; United States Holocaust Memorial Museum, Photograph #26543*. Photo from *Jürgen Stroop* Report to *Heinrich Himmler* from May 1943. Permission to use: in public domain, released to it by the United States Holocaust Memorial Museum. The right to use this work is granted to anyone for any purpose.

(9) *View of the entrance to the main camp of Auschwitz (Auschwitz I)*. The gate bears the motto "Arbeit Macht Frei" (Work makes one free). Source: Main Commission for the Investigation of Nazi War Crimes, courtesy of USHMM Photo Archives.

(10) *German Nazi death camp Auschwitz in Poland, arrival of Hungarian Jews, summer 1944*. Licensed under *Creative Commons Attribution-Share Alike 3.0 Germany* license. Attribution: Bundesarchiv, Bild 183-N0827-318 / CC-BY-SA; Permission granted to share, copy, distribute and transmit; to remix or adapt. Photographer: Ernst Hofmann or Bernhard Walte. Source: German Federal Archives, VIAF: 137346469; LCCN: n92025526; GND:

39454-3; *BnF: cb11862536s; SUDOC: 026362686; ISNI: 0000 000102166 2802; WorldCat. This image was provided to Wikimedia Commons by the German Federal Archive as part of a cooperation project. Accession number: Bild 183-NO827-318. Photo from the Auschwitz Album. (May 1944).*

(11) <u>Inspection by the Nazi party and Heinrich Himmler</u>; Reichsfuhrer der SS. Photographer, Friedrich Franz Bauer (1903-1972). Freedom granted to share – to copy, distribute and transmit the work. Licensed under <u>Creative Commons</u> Attribution-Share Alike 3.0 Germany license. Attribution: Bundesarchiv, Bild 152-11-12 / CC-BY-SA. This image was provided to Wikimedia Commons by the German Federal Archive (Deutsches Bundesarchiv) as part of a <u>cooperation project</u>.

(12) <u>Buchenwald inmate identifying Nazi guard</u>. Source: Department of Defense. This image is a work of a <u>U.S. Army</u> soldier or employee, taken or made as part of that person's official duties. As a <u>work</u> of the <u>U.S. federal government</u>, the image is in the public domain.

(13) <u>Lwów Ghetto, Poland</u>. Source: Meczenstwo Walka, Zaglada Zydów Polsce 1939-1945. Poland. Plate No. 107. Author Unknown. Polish Public Domain and USA Public Domain. Courtesy of Wikipedia

(14) <u>Burning Warsaw</u>, September 1939; Source: Wikipedia; public domain because according to the <u>Art. 3</u> of <u>copyright law of March 29, 1926</u> of the <u>Republic of Poland</u> and Art. 2 of <u>copyright law of July 10, 1952</u> of the People's <u>Republic of Poland</u>, all photographs by Polish photographers (or published for the first time in Poland or simultaneously in Poland and abroad) published without a clear copyright notice before the <u>law was changed on May 23, 1994</u> are assumed <u>public domain</u> in Poland. This work is in the public domain in the United States because it meets three requirements: 1. First <u>published</u> outside the United States (and not published in the U.S. within 30 days) 2. First published before 1978 without complying with U.S. copyright formalities or after 1978 without copyright notice 3. Was in the public domain in its home

country (Poland) on the URAA date (1 January 1996). Original source: Jerzy Piorkowski (1957) Miasto Nieujarzmione, Warsaw: Iskry, pp. 18 no ISBN

(15) <u>USS General S. D. Sturgis</u> (AP-137) at Yokohama in September 1945. Text available under the Creative Commos Attribution-Share-Alike License; source: Wikipedia; public domain; photo is more than 50 years old.

(16) <u>The Statue of Liberty: the head piece on exhibit.</u> This work is in the <u>public domain</u> in the United States, and those countries with a copyright term of life of the author plus 100 years or less. Published in 1883 in Frederic Bartholdi's Album des Travaux de Construction de la Statue Colossale de la Liberte destinee, Albert Fernique (born c. 1841, died 1898). This image is available from the United States <u>Library of Congress's</u> Prints. Source: Wikipedia

(17) <u>Adolf at the Eiffel Tower</u>, National Archives. Public Domain. From the US National Archives and Records SW68 Kochsstrasse and was seized by the US government after world war II and because it was not divested to the original copyright owner and because of the ruling in Price v. United States: US Court of Appeals, Fifth circuit, 20 November, 1995 which confirmed that under US law Heinrich Hoffman items in the national archives are not copyrighted by the original copyright owners in the US. Part of the ruling reads "The US may dispose of items that were seized during the Allied occupation of Germany as it sees fit; indeed, it has done so." This file will not be in the public domain in its home country until January 1, 2028 and should not be transferred to Wikimedia Commons until that date. Administration (NARA). Originally copyrighted by the Presse Illustrationen Hoffmann (Heinrich Hoffmann, Berlin

(18) <u>Comradeship, German and Slovakian soldiers, Komańcza, Poland 1939, Public Domain</u> archives http://portalwiedzy.onet.pl/4869,68489,1624275,2, czasopisma.htmlsource: http://portalwiedzy.onet.pl/4869,68489,1624275,2, czasopisma.html This image (or other media file) is in the public domain because its copyright has expired. <u>This file has been identified as being free of</u>

(19) <u>Warsaw Uprising</u>. *Permission to use: in the* <u>public domain</u>, *because they were released to it by the United States Holocaust Memorial Museum, The right to use this work is granted to anyone for any purpose, without any conditions, unless such conditions are required by law. Courtesy of USHMM.*

(20) <u>British female military auxiliaries handle a barrage balloon</u>. *Royal Air Force Balloon Command, 1939-1945. WAAFs hauling in a kite balloon at a coastal site. Crated and released by the Imperial War Museum on the IWM Non Commercial License, which is considered expired 50 years after their creation. CHc21007, from the collections of the Imperial War Museums. Public Domain*

49488013R00139

Made in the USA
Middletown, DE
18 October 2017